Psychology Revivals

The Case of Miss R.

Originally published in 1929 the individual psychological interpretation of this autobiography was first presented by Alfred Adler to a group of psychiatrists and pedagogues in Vienna.

The story of the development of a neurosis is told in this book. A young girl relates the fascinating story of her unhappy life, the psychologist comments on her remarks and leads the reader to an understanding of the blunders and mistakes which have made her life so full of suffering. Publication of this book in its day was intended to bring the growing interest in Adler's Individual Psychology to a wider audience. Today it can be read and enjoyed in its historical context.

The Case of Miss R.

The interpretation of a life story

Alfred Adler

LONDON AND NEW YORK

First published in 1929
by George Allen & Unwin Ltd

This edition first published in 2013 by Routledge
27 Church Road, Hove, BN3 2FA

Simultaneously published in the USA and Canada
by Routledge
711 Third Avenue, New York, NY 10017

Routledge is an imprint of the Taylor & Francis Group, an informa business

All rights reserved. No part of this book may be reprinted or reproduced
or utilised in any form or by any electronic, mechanical, or other means,
now known or hereafter invented, including photocopying and recording,
or in any information storage or retrieval system, without permission in
writing from the publishers.

Publisher's Note
The publisher has gone to great lengths to ensure the quality of this
reprint but points out that some imperfections in the original copies may
be apparent.

Disclaimer
The publisher has made every effort to trace copyright holders and
welcomes correspondence from those they have been unable to contact.

ISBN: 978-0-415-81511-6 (hbk)
ISBN3: 978-0-203-38689-7 (ebk)

THE CASE OF MISS R.

The Case of Miss R.

The Interpretation of a Life Story

By Alfred Adler

Translated by
Eleanore and Friedrich Jensen, M.D.

London
George Allen & Unwin Ltd.
40 Museum Street
W.C.
1929

PRINTED IN THE UNITED STATES OF AMERICA

CONTENTS

		PAGE
	EDITOR'S PREFACE	vii

CHAPTER

I	EARLY CHILDHOOD	3
II	ADOLESCENT DIFFICULTIES	19
III	THE DEVELOPMENT OF A NEUROSIS	32
IV	THE STYLE OF LIFE	50
V	THE JEALOUSY MANIA	75
VI	SEXUAL DEVELOPMENT	88
VII	THE PROBLEM OF LOVE	112
VIII	THE SHOCK OF SEX KNOWLEDGE	139
IX	THE MASCULINE PROTEST	167
X	A LUPUS PHOBIA	195
XI	YES! BUT—	234
XII	THE GOAL OF SUPERIORITY	273
	THE CASE OF MISS R.	304

EDITOR'S PREFACE

I

Every human problem is a social problem. Every human problem concerns not only one individual, but also the society in which that individual lives. Every person is tied by intangible threads to his community. There exists, or, rather, should exist, a mutual give and take between him and the community which lives through him and through which he lives. The community made possible his early upbringing, his education and the development of his abilities. The community enabled him to live. As a result he is inevitably faced with a set of social problems the solution of which is vitally important for establishing his physical and mental balance in which, in turn, the community is most interested. Out of the infinite number of social problems we can form three main groups: (1) interhuman relations (attitude toward fellow men, friends); (2) work (occupation or profession in the case of an adult—school in the case of a child); (3) sex (love and marriage).

Probably no one has ever solved these great, general problems completely. Such a solution would require perfect objectivity and an unbroken and unbreak-

vii

EDITOR'S PREFACE

able courage, two of the rarest and most precious of human qualities. But a complete solution of these problems is not of importance. What *is* important is the effort an individual makes honestly to meet and solve his problems, the sincerity with which he tackles them, and the courage with which he faces them. Those who draw back afraid, who make exclusively individual problems out of general social ones, to satisfy their secret lust for power, act absolutely against the community, against what Adler terms "social feeling." When that happens, we speak of a neurosis.

The story of the development of a neurosis is told in this book. A young girl relates the fascinating story of her unhappy life, the psychologist comments on her remarks and leads the reader to an understanding of the blunders and mistakes which have made her life so full of suffering. The individual psychological interpretation of this autobiography was originally presented by Dr. Adler to a group of psychiatrists and pedagogues in Vienna.

Publication in book form of this study makes it available to a larger circle of readers. The interest in Individual Psychology, not only of our professional contemporaries, but of the general public as well, is steadily growing and the radius of its influence is increasing from day to day. Yet many who have heard of this great intellectual movement are not familiar

viii

EDITOR'S PREFACE

with it; and not all those who will want to read this book will be sufficiently conversant with the system of Individual Psychology to be able to follow its contents with full understanding. With the intention of submitting this extraordinary life story to as extensive a circle of readers as possible I give a concise survey of the theory and practice of individual psychology for those who have little or no acquaintance with the fundamentals of Adlerian teaching.

The theoretical system of individual psychology was founded by the Viennese psychiatrist, Dr. Alfred Adler. Adler's conception of the structure and function of the mind in relation to the body, of the striving of all psychic expressions and activities toward a goal, and of the mutual relation between the individual psyche and the community is so illuminating and clarifying that it has brought his doctrines rapidly to the fore in modern psychology.

Adler proceeds from the fact that bodily defects are not only to be considered as signs of physical deterioration but also frequently give rise to attempts at compensation and overcompensation. As soon as there is a physical disturbance the body attempts to compensate for it. Since every bodily disturbance makes an impression on the mind a mental striving sets in concurrently with the compensatory efforts of the body, with the aim of overcoming or, at least, making up for this defect in some way or other. The body,

EDITOR'S PREFACE

for instance, may not be able to make a physical compensation for defective vision, but there may be a mental compensation in the form of greater clarity in thought or improved inner visualization (that is, recapturing with greater accuracy the details of things seen). The bodily defect, recording itself on the psyche as well, may direct the mind to an interest in the visible side of life, as it were; just as a defective ear may increase interest in and perfect the comprehension of sound. This would be a mental or psychic compensation. If there is no possibility of compensating for the physical defect by physical means there still remains a purely psychical compensation in the form of greater clarity in thought, or an ability to recapture the outer world in correct detail before one's inner eye. This can frequently be observed among those whose vision has become weak. In most cases, however, a bodily as well as a mental compensation is inaugurated.

The biological law of compensation, as a phenomenon of all living matter, plays just as important a role on purely psychical as on physical ground. It is the motor of psychic preservation and development; the propelling force of the motor is life itself.

Adler has termed such defects "organ inferiorities." According to him every inferiority produces an urge for betterment, for an adjustment to the de-

EDITOR'S PREFACE

mands of the environment which will compensate for the inferiority. One can, however, think of inferiorities which are to be found in a healthy body and normal mind and which arise solely out of the fact that this body and mind are comparatively less developed than the majority of human beings. This is the situation which every child meets in early life.

On account of his limited abilities, every healthy child feels himself inferior, consciously or unconsciously, in a world of gigantic and apparently self-sufficient adults. That is the relative feeling of inferiority which is compensated under favorable conditions by a striving for recognition on the "useful side of life." The feeling of inferiority or insecurity, like every unpleasant feeling, requires a quick, compensatory balancing. A feeling of superiority or security obviously compensates for a feeling of inferiority. The child learns this by experience and gradually establishes a fixed but fictive goal of superiority or security which, according to his own unconscious interpretation or evaluation of his position and faculties, lies more or less close to reality.

One must not assume that the child thinks of such a goal in conscious, logical terms as we do when we race to win a prize or struggle to attain distinction. In only a fraction of cases is the goal ever verbalized in a childish way by expressing the wish to become like the father, or a king or a policeman, which, in

EDITOR'S PREFACE

the child's world, are always dominating positions. One can merely draw the conclusion from the child's actions that he is striving for a perfection which will compensate for his inferiorities. He may never have spoken of these inferiorities and may not even be conscious of them, but he feels them as surely as we can observe them and the mechanism he sets up to compensate for them. Conscious inferiority thoughts are on an entirely different level from the unconscious feeling of inferiority, and serve an entirely different purpose.

When this feeling of inferiority is aroused, he begins to train for the attainment of this fictive goal by employing his psychic qualities, such as sensitivity, volition, perception, memory, and so on, as useful instruments, and develops them in conformity with his interpretation of his own situation. The sum total, in a cross section, of all forms of expression of an individual is called his behavior pattern; his method of approaching his personal goal of superiority is termed his style of life. When we discover the goal of an individual, we are then able to trace his behavior pattern and style of life and to disclose and modify his entire life scheme.

The most satisfactory compensation for the feeling of inferiority is the development of courage, objectivity and social feeling. An individual compensating satisfactorily, approaches life in a sincere and

EDITOR'S PREFACE

fearless manner, tries to solve his problems and accomplish his tasks as they come along, and adapts himself to the smaller or larger community in which he lives. He trains in an upward direction, toward a superiority which is concerned with progress, improvement, adjustment to the world; in short, with useful things. Adler calls this "the striving on the useful side of life." What is useful? The shortest definition I can frame is that everything is useful that promotes life, everything useless that prohibits life. Life, however, is not only the living of a single individual; life means the living of all with whom an individual comes in contact, physically and mentally. Striving for useful superiority, that is, for the promotion of life, therefore, means the promotion of all living things or, in other words, the development of social feeling. Just as courage grows out of the successful accomplishment of tasks, social feeling grows out of devotion to others, assisting others, out of firm belief in and appreciation of others. An attitude so oriented cannot be egotistical, egocentric; it simply has to be objective to be true. Objectivity is developed along with courage and social feeling in approaching the great problems of life, that is, work, social relations, and love.

However, if the child has a heavier burden to bear as a result of physical defects ("organ inferiorities") or unfavorable social and environmental circum-

EDITOR'S PREFACE

stances, the normal relative inferiority feeling increases to an absolute one. Again compensation sets in, this time, however, with all the more force the longer and more deeply the feeling of inferiority has been sensed. The visible result of it is a more and more intense striving for that feeling which is believed by the individual to be the only sure remedy for the inferiority sting. Such a person will either accomplish something extraordinary provided he has sufficient courage to direct his intense drive into useful channels (great artists, scientists and explorers); or he will accomplish little or nothing, by avoiding in a cowardly fashion the difficult road of a useful striving for recognition, and choosing the seemingly easier path to power at any price. Persons like these strive with all their might for superiority, for triumphs over and the suppression of their fellow human beings because of purely egotistical reasons; in fact, quite obviously, in order to elevate their own shattered self-esteem, regardless of how much pain and trouble their conduct deviations cost them. If all the energy and skill spent in attaining that sort of goal were used in useful ways, neurotic persons would be far beyond the average of their more courageous and more social contemporaries.

In an organized civilization an attempt to overcome all assumed competitors by a fictitious superiority has to fail finally, save perhaps in the small,

EDITOR'S PREFACE

restricted circle of a family. Thus its results are uselessness in a generally social sense, and, instead of the development of courage, objectivity and social feeling, a constantly increasing discouragement, egocentricity and asocial or antisocial feelings (criminals) accompanied by feelings of inadequacy, insufficiency, dissatisfaction and disgust. The futility of all neurotic efforts to master, without an appropriate justification, the world in which we live, induces such individuals to retreat farther and farther until they reach that vast region where responsibility for their activities is no longer required. I mean the region of disease.

The sick are exempted from duties, the sick are irresponsible, especially when they are supposed to be mentally sick. To use the cloak of disease as a means to attain one's goal is a dangerous deception, for the patient himself, who does it unconsciously, as well as for every one who is taken in by it.

That is the way of all neuroses (including common nervousness, nervous breakdowns, neurasthenia, hysteria, delinquency, perversions, addiction to drugs, etc.) and psychoses for whose recognition and description, the theory, and for whose prophylaxis and treatment, the practice of individual psychology serves. No one is compelled to follow one road or the other. According to Adler, it is unnecessary to believe in inherited or inheritable character traits. Every

EDITOR'S PREFACE

one can achieve everything in life, even his own misfortune. For the alleged neurotic disease is nothing but the price which the cowardly, asocial egotist has to pay for offending the "logic of life."

II

To make more easily comprehensible the neurotic life scheme and the particular form of nervous disorder discussed in this book, Adler's conceptions of the construction of neuroses in general will be delineated in somewhat more detail in the following paragraphs. What happens in a nervous disorder?

The feeling of inferiority, when compensation takes a neurotic direction, drives the patient to achieve as absolute a domination as possible over his surroundings. The disorder with all its arrangements serves different purposes: (1) to be used as an alibi for having evaded the problems of life and as an excuse for having refused to assume responsibility; (2) to serve as a cloak when life withholds the longed-for triumphs; (3) to be able to postpone decisions; and (4) to throw a strong light upon achieved ambition because it has been attained despite the disorder.

The neurotic thus has the fictive goal to strive for in order to make safe his ostensible superiority. His actions are directed from this point and maintain a typical pattern. The compulsion to secure superiority is so powerful that every psychic phenomenon con-

EDITOR'S PREFACE

stitutes, aside from its outward appearance, an attempt to get rid of the feeling of weakness or inadequacy, to gain the height, to rise from below to above. In order to create the desired arrangement and safety from defeat in overcautiously preparing to experience and comprehend the world's events, the neurotic has recourse to a number of rules and auxiliary formulas in life which, in accordance with his infantile attitude, form a primitive, antithetic scheme ("falsified apperception"). He perceives only those qualities which correspond to the "below" and "above" in his scheme, and tries to relate these qualities to the more easily comprehensible contrast of masculine-feminine. He endeavors to force violently onto a masculine track traits in his character condemned as feminine, such as obedience, cowardice, tenderheartedness, passive behavior, incapabilities of all sort. He develops hate, cruelty, stubbornness, egotism and other tendencies which are supposed to secure him triumphs ("masculine protest"). This is an aggressive protest, but the aggression may also be expressed by passive means when the neurotic attempts to score by his weakness, forcing his environment to be subservient to him. Moreover, this strategy enables him to escape dreaded decisions with ostensibly sufficing reasons.

When an individual feels that the development of "masculine" qualities in life is necessary but im-

EDITOR'S PREFACE

possible for him, he will avoid the struggles and problems of life, fearing he may be accused of appearing "feminine." "In such a case one will always find a striving that deviates from the direct road and, because of constant fear of mistakes and defeat, tries to take safe detours."

The neurotic purposiveness is based upon two unconscious premises: (1) all human relationships are struggles for supremacy; (2) the female sex is subordinate, inferior, and its reaction serves as a measure of masculine strength. These two premises can be found in men as well as in women and mutilate all human relationships. A desirable frankness is replaced by constant dissatisfaction. The neurotic symptom represents the excessive greed for superiority; it produces a semblance of a victory over the environment. To understand the language of symptoms is, according to Adler, one of the chief tasks of psychotherapeutic endeavor.

The neurotic's style of life and the arrangement of his particular neurosis are closely connected. The feeling of inferiority, arising from actual facts, then inflated and later on maintained for certain tendencies, drives the patient to set his goal in early childhood far beyond all human proportions. In order to intrench this goal he surrounds himself with a widely ramified net of precautions, all of which tend to maintain his superiority. In a case of washing-

xviii

EDITOR'S PREFACE

compulsion the goal in view is to be the cleanest human being on earth, an entirely useless enterprise, of course. What really happens is that this superhumanly clean person neglects the simplest duties of social life (including cleanliness), avoids responsibilities, exerts pressure on others, retreats from reality with many excuses, but still retains a well-fed feeling of superiority ("No one is as immaculately clean as I am . . .") —at least in the small circle of the family.

The neurotic scheme of life is rigid and compulsory and can be traced only when one succeeds in comprehending the general and special goals of the patient. Somebody, for example, will use a fear to leave his house (agoraphobia) to raise his own prestige in his family and to force his environment to obey him, by unconsciously connecting the thought of being left alone, of going out alone, with fear-producing images of personal misfortunes or accidents to others. (Refer to the fear of lupus, chapt. X.) Every possible defeat is anticipated and exaggerated by connecting it with thoughts of death, illness, or all sorts of mischief. Thus the neurotic manages to escape a useful life by establishing pessimistic trains of thought.

On the other hand, the neurotic frequently displays extreme expectations. Followed, of a surety, by just as extreme disappointments, these expectations

EDITOR'S PREFACE

are designed to justify the patient in producing all kinds of demonstrative emotions, such as hate, grief, sullenness, etc. Disappointed expectations are most frequently seen in cases where the patient wants to avoid his sexual problems. Some men, to use a frequent example, divide all women into two classes: madonnas and prostitutes (falsified apperception!). The madonnas are unattainably high, the prostitutes despicably low. If such a man becomes acquainted with one of his unattainably high madonnas, his illusions are soon demolished since women are human beings and not madonnas. The disappointment, following such an unwarranted assumption, proves him ostensibly right and permits him merely to keep on wishing. "As long as some one only wishes, nothing is going to happen," says Adler.

Some one may take the greatest pains imaginable to attain the alleged goal of his wishes. That is his justification. But since he is a victim of his subconscious, fictive goal of superiority, the arrangements he makes to approach the rational goal of normal sexual relations will prove impossible for that purpose, for these arrangements really tend to preserve the fictitious goal of superiority. Normal love relations, however, are impossible as long as one person believes he must be or is superior or inferior to another. Thus he is excused and his subconscious goal of superiority is not endangered. Adler has illus-

EDITOR'S PREFACE

trated the neurotic contradiction in the following way: The desire to attain a normal goal is designated by the patient's saying "Yes," the actually effective fictive goal with its prearranged consequences expressed by an excusing "But." The sequence of "Yes-But" typifies the pace of the neurotic. Example: A man wants to marry, BUT he does not find a girl. He tries to meet the "right" girl, but does not succeed. That is possible—for a while at least. However, for twenty years he does not succeed in finding a woman to marry—and is "safe." Adler calls the yes-but attitude the shortest and most cogent definition of a neurosis.

A third means to escape defeat and inferiority feelings consists in anticipatory sensations, emotions and perceptions, ominous "identifications which, in relation to dangerous situations, have a preparing, warning or stimulating effect and which occur in dreams and all forms of neurotic delusions" (Adler). The girl in this book anticipates in graphic fashion a whole string of misfortunes in order to escape the dreaded problems of life and to maintain her dominating position in an injudicious, pampering family, no matter how high the price of suffering was for all concerned.

Psychic treatment, therefore, has three essential tasks: (1) the disclosure of the neurotic system or style of life; (2) gradual encouragement in facing

EDITOR'S PREFACE

reality; and (3) redirecting toward useful goals in social life as described above. The success of the treatment depends as well upon the co-operation and sincere efforts of the patient. The tendency to assume the rôle of the superior induces him to try to defeat his physician at every opportunity. In order not to have to change his goal the neurotic will do everything possible to forestall a cure by arranging disturbing emotions, falling in love with the physician, or exhibiting an inimical attitude toward him. The physician has continuously to investigate and explain the arrangements and constructions of the neurotic mode of life until the patient, his position made untenable, gives them up. Frequently, to be sure, he substitutes new mechanisms, still better concealed. Step by step the patient's unattainably high goal and its purposive, constraining consequences have to be unveiled. The sincere, objective and courageous attempt to approach the three main problems (social contact, work and love) leads to a useful and harmonious life.

FRIEDRICH JENSEN, M.D.

THE CASE OF MISS R.

CHAPTER I

EARLY CHILDHOOD

WE usually learn from books, whether we want to or not. At least we hope to discover in them some answer to our own questions and some solution to our own difficulties. This is especially true when we pick up a book which occupies itself with the problems of our psychic life. What other purpose can the study of psychology have if it does not give us some practical help in our difficulties, or at least make it possible to help ourselves?

In this book I attempt to give to the reader an insight into the methods and technique of individual psychology. This art of treating the human mind is demonstrable to a definite degree and indubitably open to every one whose own mind does not lack the deeper insight into the connective unity of human life. We must know the chirographic symbols of our speech in order to read the language we speak. Just, as with this knowledge we can read an otherwise strange language, so must we know the symbols of the soul in order to read a life.

THE CASE OF MISS R.

We often read biographies; many are filled with dramatic and exciting life stories. Most of them have to do either with persons whose form of life or attainment was in some way unusual or dramatic. It is often the activity of the individual or the literary form which makes the biography interesting. Here I take a life story, which, though it is vivid and colorful, is nevertheless the story of a girl of ordinary station and no particular accomplishment. That the psychological side of biography may well be the most fascinating, I believe this story will illustrate.

The art of individual psychology is based on knowledge and common sense. Only to those laboring under psychological prejudices will it appear peculiar, strange or tricky. In this book I proceed as I do in my office when I listen to a patient's story for the first time. The comments on the story are based on no more knowledge of the facts than are available to the reader. With intention, I proceed extemporaneously and tell the story as it was given to me, reading it for the first time as I give my interpretation. With every sentence, with every word of the patient, I consider: What is the real meaning of what she is saying? What is this person's attitude toward life? What do her words mean in the light of her deeds? How does she meet the demands life makes of her? How does she behave toward her fellow human beings? How does she perform her duties (or

EARLY CHILDHOOD

fail to perform them)? Does she tend to reality or illusion?

Provided with the framework of this story, the gaps of which we gradually fill out from our own experiences, we observe this girl endeavoring to achieve a complete expression of her personality and to master the problems of living. We go back to the very early years, because it is my belief that the development of a human being is largely determined in the first four or five years.

I now begin the story of Miss R. It is as unknown to me as it is to you, and I comment as I read.

I remember that father frequently asked me. . . .

It is worth while inquiring: Why not the mother? "Father" has a special significance. This child, a girl, was much more strongly attached to her father than to her mother. What does that mean? From the fact that the child prefers her father we can conclude that he must be a tender-hearted man. A child is first attached to her mother. That is natural and easily understood. The mother represents to the child her first connection with the world. The mother helps her and usually pampers her. The second phase sets in later when the child has become somewhat more independent. She seeks to attach herself to those persons who treat her best; that is to say, she either remains attached to her mother or turns to others.

THE CASE OF MISS R.

Here the mother had started to pamper the child but apparently could not compete with the father in the child's attention.

Do you feel well? Does anything hurt you?

The girl begins her story with a childhood remembrance. Psychological experience has shown us that childhood remembrances are not as meaningless as we had formerly supposed. From the endless store of childhood memories which each one of us has, only a few are carried over to maturity. This very fact should emphasize the importance of these remembered impressions. And so when an adult tells us of an early remembrance (it matters little whether it is the first or not) which is particularly clear to him, we are able to interpret from it the speaker's personal attitude toward life. This is, in essence, the attitude he has retained up to the moment of telling, even should that be twenty, thirty or forty years later. If his attitude toward life has changed in the course of years, the childhood memories which occur to him before and after such a change will differ.

Possibly a concrete example will serve to clarify this point. Suppose you are in a strange city for the first time and are being taken over a long road from the station to the house of your host. You will, of course, have seen a great many things on the way. On arriving home you are asked what you remember

EARLY CHILDHOOD

and you may answer, a monument in the park, some flowers in a window, a delicatessen store, a horse being whipped, the shrill whistle of a factory, the severe jolting of the taxi or what not. But because you were being led and at the same time had confidence in your leader, you would pay little attention to the route. On the other hand, were you alone in the city and forced to find your own way on foot, you would note landmarks and guides and direction and be able to describe in exact detail the way over which you had come.

A child is alone in a strange city depending for guidance on its mother, or father, or whoever the preferred person is. It will remember only those things which make a sharp impression because they fit into an already established scheme of existence or attitude toward life.

We endeavor, therefore, to draw some conclusions from the early remembrances of this girl. These conclusions are still further corroborated in that the girl thought the facts of sufficient importance to put them at the beginning of her story.

Her father must have been an extraordinarily soft, weak man, and the girl must have been a very spoiled child. We infer that this girl will always see to it that she is pampered. She will always want to be the center of attraction and she will constantly try to draw attention to herself. Difficulties arise as soon as such a

THE CASE OF MISS R.

child comes in contact with other persons who do not give her the same attention she receives from the person who pampers her. In such a case we find a strong tendency to reject, an aversion to strangers, a critical attitude toward and lack of interest in other persons, and a reluctance to adjust herself to new situations. This pampering may be based on her father's nature, or she may be in an exceptional position. She is either an only child, grown up under especially unfavorable circumstances, or she may be the only girl among boys, or the youngest child. Some one or other of her organs may also be deficient in functioning.

I never felt quite well.

We cannot accept literally the statements of our patients. Such statements must not influence us as they influence the patients themselves. What this girl means to say is: I was a sickly child.

I always had some temperature (that is hard to believe) *and my hands were so hot and dry that I had to moisten them with my tongue.*

We know that there are better ways of moistening the hands; moreover, in a case of fever the tongue is also dry. She may have used her tongue to moisten her hands for quite another purpose than the one she mentions. One can frequently observe that children use their tongues for purposes of which the

EARLY CHILDHOOD

persons around them disapprove. Her father probably did not like it and the girl has thus drawn her father's attention to herself. We are therefore able to note another trait: the girl has a strong inclination to secure and strengthen her central position by misbehaving.

My father told me later that my life had hung by a thread.

Many healthy people have been told this. My life also "hung by a thread." Later on I saw that this was not true. In most cases such a remark is an exaggeration which serves to make the speaker or writer more important. He who feels it necessary to exaggerate, must, in the first instance, feel himself inferior. The girl does not tell what ailed her. We learn only that she was a fragile child who did not eat very well but apparently only because she had been spoiled. We know the practice among children of refusing to eat; it serves the purpose of drawing attention to themselves.

I never had any appetite, never liked to eat anything. I could not stand the taste of food and I chewed the morsels as if they were paper or grass. I remember vaguely that my parents complained of me to our physician. The only thing that had any taste was mother's milk; I am said to have fought desperately every attempt to wean me.

THE CASE OF MISS R.

It is striking that this girl writes extremely well in spite of the fact that she did not get very far in school.

Thus I remained a nursing infant for an extraordinarily long time, in fact, for five years.

That is quite improbable. But even if it were only for two years, we can assume that this girl was deeply attached to her mother. This confirms our previous statement; namely, that the attachment to her father represents the second phase. Perhaps incorrect treatment in the child's infancy was one of the reasons for withdrawing from her mother. It is a tragedy when a two-year old child is weaned.

I can still see my mother's beautiful white breast in front of me.

It is not so certain that the child has remembered this; one can form such images subsequently. Again we have to bear in mind that such an image serves certain purposes which seem to have nothing to do with the image. We have found up to the present that the girl has been spoiled and, as a consequence, makes other people serve her. Her interest is directed toward the devotion of others to herself. It is painful to her to have to relinquish her mother's breast since much tenderness and attention accompany such an easy method of nourishment. This girl still thinks that there was nothing wrong with her upbringing.

EARLY CHILDHOOD

I felt ashamed. When we had visitors, I used to whisper in mother's ear, "Come, let me drink." Then she had to seat herself where no one could see us.

The child therefore knew that it was a disgrace.

When mother went to visit the relatives of her dead first husband, she did not know what to do with me. My older sister was willing to take me on her breast, but I said: "It is not the same as when mother takes me. You are blond and mother is dark. I don't like blond hair."

We can observe from this remark what trifles and superficialities play a part in preference for or rejection of a person. Some one is agreeable to us because he has eyes like one of our friends; another we spurn because he speaks like a teacher whom we hated. We like a girl because her hair is the same color, her complexion or her figure the same as our mother's. Often we do not know by what delicate, undetectable mechanisms our sympathies are aroused. Even those persons whom we select to love and marry have, in many cases, appealed to us so strongly only because they seem to bear a superficial, usually physical resemblance to the former recipient of our affection. In such cases the connection can remain completely obscured, and usually does.

As we now know, this girl was very much attached to her mother in early childhood and stresses dis-

THE CASE OF MISS R.

tinguishing characteristics which are of no importance to us.

I myself had dark hair.

She speaks about hair for the second time. She places a peculiar emphasis on hair.

My father had my hair cut low on my forehead. At that time I wore a blue cape with red lining and I wanted to have a hat. Every time we passed a store, I cried, "Hat! Cape!"

Vanity developed early and a great penchant for externals. There was a strong evaluation of beauty.

They could not get me away from the stores. Finally my mother had to make a detour around those shop windows.

The child has an influence over her mother strong enough to compel her to use tricks.

Before mother took me out, she would ask my father what dress she should put on me.

The mother is likewise interested in the child's appearance; it is easily comprehensible how vanity is instilled in the girl.

I was very happy about my first shoes; they were hardly put on my feet when I opened the door and tried to run away with them.

EARLY CHILDHOOD

That is an attempt to insure their possession. Her father is a tailor; the whole family is prone to appreciate the external. This is therefore not an inherited trait but lies in the atmosphere of the house.

There were many buttons in the house; I played games with them which I invented myself. They were my money.

The child is prematurely interested in work and money.

Furthermore I liked to play with silk pads. I used to cut holes in them through which I put the arms of my doll.

Preparation for the occupation of dressmaking.

I liked still more to play with a beer bottle.

We know that children would rather employ their own fantasy than play with mechanical toys. . . . The child learns by imitation. That, however, she can do only when she identifies herself with others, when she plays a rôle which she has assumed from her father and mother. She imitates her father when she patterns a dress.

I rummaged in the drawers, busied myself with locks.

The child has had great freedom in playing with what she wanted.

13

THE CASE OF MISS R.

My favorite occupation was talking to myself. I could imitate somebody for hours.

She imitates tailoring and talking, also the doctor and the cook. A logical profession for a child who trains at an early age to identify herself with others or with a rôle is that of an actress. Many people are unconsciously prepared for certain professions which they never choose because they do not know anything about their early preparation.

I also imitated the baker. My bakery shop was a drawer with remains of bread which I took to bed with me at night.

Intense desire to represent something; the child wants to be a baker even at night.

Later on I played teacher, using eye-glasses just as my teacher did in school. I cut glasses for myself from red parchment. Father's catalogues and note-books represented school books and the back rest of the sofa was the blackboard.

We see the stage of Shakespeare.

I threatened the disobedient children and shouted so loudly that my father told me not to get so excited.

Another method of securing her father's attention.

I played workman with the coffee grinder.

14

EARLY CHILDHOOD

Imagination and imitation strongly developed.

There were two old people in our house who sold coal. I piled up wood in their store and sometimes ate dinner with them. The food I ate there I would not have touched at home; for instance, sauerkraut and meat balls. But at their house I liked to eat everything.

Refusing to eat is an attempt to draw attention to oneself by protesting against an ostensibly important function. When one is hungry one eats again. As soon as a child notices that it can secure no attention through such useless manœuvres and that it harms only itself in not receiving any attention it will abandon this trick.

The coal dealer asked me whom I wanted to marry. I always answered, "My father."

This might be thought an incestuous wish. When one considers, however, that this child does not know anything about sexual relations, it is highly probable that the girl's desire to marry her father is only possible because her relation to him is completely asexual.

I loved my father very much. I was even jealous of him.

If jealousy were always an expression of sex love then we should be wrong. But there also exists a

THE CASE OF MISS R.

jealousy originating in a striving for power. It is quite possible that all jealousy really springs from a striving for superiority. He only can be jealous who feels himself inferior to the one of whom he is jealous—weaker, less intelligent, insufficient. He believes that his abilities and mentality are not adequate to compete honestly with a rival and he attempts to exert pressure through jealousy; that is to say, to demonstrate his power. The fact that jealousy is to be found so frequently in love relations does not justify its being classed as an exclusive expression of sexual love. Jealousy is very often a matter of prestige.

When my mother caressed my father, I frequently interfered, stroked his hair, rolled up his shirt sleeves and kissed his arms.

I do not believe that this is an expression of sexual love. Any explanation based on sexual consideration is fallacious.

When I was naughty, my mother would threaten to order a brother or sister from the stork, and I would cry, "I'll throw him out."

Here the jealousy caused by a striving for superiority is plainly evident.

I held the storks in great respect. I admired them and could not understand how storks could bring

EARLY CHILDHOOD

the babies, who looked so stupid. I heard later on in school that babies came out of the belly. How they started, I did not know. I thought one simply ordered them when one married.

The girl has not the slightest idea about the origin of human beings.

When father travelled, he always brought me a present, a toy or a book. Then he took me on his lap and read to me. After twenty-one years I can remember how my father had to read to me. I impressed the words on my memory. When I noticed that people read in the café, I took my book with me and memorized the paragraphs aloud. Two women wondered that such a little child could read. Father sent postcards; I always received two and they were always prettier than the others. However, I could not rest until every one had given me his or her card.

She wants to have everything, a phenomenon of the increased inferiority feeling.

On account of my sickly constitution, everybody was submissive to me.

This girl will put her sickliness into the service of her striving for superiority by the way she behaves.

I was sick very often, suffering frequently from tonsillitis.

17

THE CASE OF MISS R.

"The mountains are in labor; a ridiculous mouse is about to be born."

I remember being brought to the children's hospital. I disliked having some one look into my throat and I was afraid of the tongue depressor.

There is a tendency to reject the doctor. The pampered child is anxious to be an object of pity.

I was afraid I would suffocate.

One can imagine how this girl will behave in later life.

CHAPTER II

ADOLESCENT DIFFICULTIES

*F*OR *one year I had whooping cough. For the first six months it grew steadily worse and it was a year before I was finally over it.*

Whooping cough does not last twelve months. When no lung complications or other illnesses set in afterwards, whooping cough is over in three to four months at the most. Since no mention is made of such complications, the only conclusion to be drawn is that the child voluntarily retained the symptoms of whooping cough for her own purposes. What could be the reason? Sick people demand and usually receive much more attention, care and tenderness than those who are healthy. Sick people are helpless, in need of protection and nursing. It does not matter what their age is; they usually act like children again.

As we know, the small child lives an egotistically happy existence, without responsibility and at the cost of his fellow human beings. One might believe this condition desirable for everybody. That is not the case, or we should probably all be sick or pretend to be. The normal human being is much too

THE CASE OF MISS R.

much attracted by diverse interests and pleasures to like being taken care of and ordered about longer than is necessary. On the other hand, there are individuals who anticipate too great difficulties in life and who do not, consequently, develop themselves from healthy human beings to useful ones. Such persons frequently regard illness as a suitable means to achieve without effort the semblance of superiority. That is ruling through weakness. It is obvious that such persons feel inadequate or too weak to enter into competition with their healthy fellow creatures. (Persons with inferiority feelings are always inclined to look upon life as a fight in some form or other in which they must always be ahead of the others.) Driven by this feeling of inferiority or insufficiency in comparison to others, they seek a way out which will procure for them the triumph of being first, at least in the small circle of their intimates. They seize upon sickness as a welcome means to attain such tinsel triumphs. While they are training their symptoms they are also training for an ostensible superiority. That goes on until they find the cost of their cowardly attitude becoming too high, and they simply discard their symptoms. Frequently the discontinuance of one symptom is merely the signal for the acquisition of a new one. Or they have arrived at the point where, hopelessly lost in the mazes of their vari-

ADOLESCENT DIFFICULTIES

ous strivings, and completely discouraged, they appear before the doctor.

Even if we knew nothing else about this girl, we might infer from the assertion that the whooping cough lasted twelve months that she felt sufficiently inferior to drag out a sickness as long as she could. We understand this girl's inferiority feeling very well since we learned from some former remarks that she had been badly spoiled. Pampered children always suffer from a strong feeling of inferiority because they grow up like hot-house plants, and therefore dread the raw reality of life as soon as they are brought in contact with it. But not only that. In order to retain their favorable position of security they will purposely exaggerate the harshness and difficulties of life and thereby lessen their courage. Their feeling of inferiority, which is nothing more nor less than the result of a wrong interpretation, becomes absolute and the urge to rule, as compensation for the inferiority sting, is intensified in direct ratio to the deepening feeling of inferiority. Thus the deplorable retreat of the neurotic is developed out of cowardice and excessive lust for power.

One night I had such a choking fit that I wanted to climb out of the window in my stupor.

Exaggeration.

THE CASE OF MISS R.

I was so weak that I could hardly walk; I was brought into the open air in a wheel-chair. The people avoided me.

A pampered child does not care about that.

The children were hurried away from me.

Children are always taken away from such a sight.

Since the doctor had recommended humid air, we made excursions to the old Danube. I often vomited when coughing. After each fit I fell back in my chair and was as if dead.

The pampered child seizes every opportunity to make a strong impression with her coughing spells. The more the child is pampered, the more severe the disease seems to be. The child does not want to give up her whooping cough.

At times I heard my father say that he would commit suicide if anything were to happen to me.

Her father is a dreamer. This girl knows that her father has a great affection for her. She is conscious of her power over him.

His eyes were always resting on me with an expression of sorrow. . . . At night my father also washed me.

The spoiled child does not do anything herself; every one around her is employed.

ADOLESCENT DIFFICULTIES

I was afraid of water and always struggled against being washed.

That is not innate; no peculiarity. This child makes herself important with everything. Washing becomes a rite. She shows her father that he has to make an effort with her.

The worst was cutting my toe nails.

The same tendency as refusing to eat. Children who make trouble are spoiled children.

Then I started to whine as if my toes were being cut off. I also hated having my hair washed.

All children act alike when something does not suit them or when they face situations which are strange or disagreeable to them. They brush them aside; they revolt. Either they ridicule the new situation or struggle against it. Many even have temper tantrums. The supposition that such bad behavior lies hidden in the collective unconscious of mankind (Jung) is quite unnecessary. Just as superfluous is Freud's assumption that conduct deviations prove that the development of mankind is repeated in every single human being.

When Lina (her sister) *washed her feet, I crept to her on all fours and lifted her skirts to see what was beneath them.*

THE CASE OF MISS R.

Early sexual curiosity.

From the time I outgrew the perambulator, I slept in my parents' bed. I went to bed every night in the following way:

Spoiled children make trouble when going to sleep, especially when the child is no longer attached to the mother. Going to bed is painstakingly described.

First my father had to take me in his arms, dance around with me and sing a song which ran: "None of the fairies is as pretty and fine as you, dear little darling of mine."

Appreciation of her prettiness by her father.

He had to shake the pillows, arrange them correctly, and cover me.

Pampered child.

I lay beside my mother; when she was away, I lay beside father. He gave me a little bell like one used on Christmas Eve so that I could ring it when I wanted my mother. I rang the little bell, father turned on the light, Lina rushed to my bed. Then I fell asleep again.

The anxiety that children have during the night is called pavor nocturnus. Such anxiety is a purposeful symptom, like the ringing of the little bell her father gave her. What happens when the bell tinkles?

ADOLESCENT DIFFICULTIES

Her devotees are awakened and must hurry to her side. She assures herself of the attention and obedience of her servants. She feels her power, and, satisfied, falls asleep again. A child neglects certain functions (such as that which leads to bed-wetting) for the same end, to attract attention. Such neglect is like the little bell, a sign that the child wants attention, and it is continued as long as its real purpose has not been detected.

Psychoanalysts regard pavor nocturnus as the result of a child's having witnessed sexual intercourse between its parents. That shows a lack of humor.

The anxiety state appears in many forms of varying severity. Often it is only a slight disturbance in sleep, sometimes a paroxysm of fear, according to the strength of the child's striving for superiority. The intensity of the symptom's manifestation is irrelevant. What is important is that the symptom always follows the same rigid scheme—to attract notice by disturbing others.

We had two boarders. One of them was a Hungarian barber by the name of Nagy. He limped. I was afraid of him. He wanted to pet me but I ran away and hid myself.

There is an early instilled fear of physical defects. That is intelligible considering the fact that the child has attached herself to one person. Such a fear is

THE CASE OF MISS R.

sometimes nourished by the environment. Parents frequently pull their children away from the sight of a beggar. Thus they create fear and aversion instead of pity. Our civilization is cruel.

One day I was sitting on the couch with my doll. The barber came into the room and stroked me. I became frightened, fell down and remained as stiff as if I were having a tetanic fit. Father and Lina were in agony.

This seems to have been a swoon which becomes intelligible when we remember that the girl resents every person except her father, especially if the other person looks peculiar or strange. I knew a child, a year and a half old, who cried bitterly when he saw a homely or badly dressed person. In this case not only is the high esteem of beauty responsible, but also the unaccustomed sight, this the more so since spoiled children are more prone to notice unusual scenes.

Once in a while a man with a clubfoot came to the café where we sat. I trembled, tried to hide myself, buried my face in my father's lap. Sometimes he had to take me home.

Always making trouble. While the parents sit quietly in a café, the girl gives them something to do. She forces them to go away with her.

ADOLESCENT DIFFICULTIES

Every now and then we visited a restaurant where a military band played. As soon as the conductor raised his baton and the music suddenly began, I got a shock. My father had to leave the restaurant with me.

She occupies her father. It is the same pattern. We can gather something else from these examples. Her memories are chiefly of optical impressions. She mentions once or twice remembering audible impressions when she tells how her father had to sing to her, and again in her last remark about the military band. She probably belongs to the visual as well as the auditory type. What do these classifications mean?

It has long been known that many people are especially and preferably interested in visible things. They remember far better things they have seen than what they have heard, and they are better able to retain those impressions which have been *visually* striking. We call this the visual type.

On the other hand another type uses its sense of hearing for the perception of the outside world and remembers primarily things heard. That is the auditory type.

Most people belong to both types with a slightly greater emphasis placed on one or the other.

A third type is what we call the motor type. People of this type seem to have a noticeably strong impulse to bodily movement.

THE CASE OF MISS R.

We have learned from long observation and considerable study that the type to which an individual belongs is not mere chance. In very many cases it can be conclusively proven that the type to which a person has elected to train himself represents in reality a compensation for a defect in the functioning of one or more of the five senses, or a deficiency in the organs of motion (limbs). A congenital or acquired inferiority of the eyes, for example, calls forth a compensatory endeavor to overcome the inferiority in spite of the inadequate eyes and therewith starts a permanent training in the direction of the visual. Even if the original organic inferiority vanishes completely in later years, the individual still pursues the same training pattern. The difficulties in surmounting the inferiority must have made an ineradicable impression to be able to determine the kind of memories carried over to adulthood.

What I have just said regarding the visual type holds just as good for the auditory and motor types, where disturbances of the respective organs form the foundation for the different training patterns.

I was also terribly frightened when I found a feather in my bed. Then I yelled as if it were a monster.

Anxiety is well known in the history of the pampered child. We notice how she arranges for this

ADOLESCENT DIFFICULTIES

mood in advance by being interested in everything which can arouse anxiety. Other psychological schools explain the phenomenon of anxiety otherwise. The psychoanalysts, for instance, claim that anxiety is induced by repressed sexual desire. It may be that fear can result from such repression, but perhaps it is just the other way around and the anxiety is the emotion repressed. The advanced psychoanalysts attempted to take this into account by asserting that every anxiety springs from the original anxiety accompanying the act of birth. We, however, are of the opinion that birth is a situation in which so intelligent a function as anxiety is not in place. Our method of tracing the purpose and effect of an emotional expression has brought to our notice that anxiety is a first-rate means by which to rule others. The girl summons her father to help her overcome her anxiety. In this life story we hear continually of anxious moments. She employs every one and everything in her constant mania to dominate.

When I was five years old, the following happened. While I was playing with my doll, I felt myself forced mentally to call my parents and God bad names, such as dirty slut, lousy dog, and so on.

How does this reaction of hate arise in the child? The psychoanalysts would say that it is an outburst of innate sadism.

THE CASE OF MISS R.

When we consider this more carefully, we come to the conclusion that the girl is a spoiled child who fights desperately against the demolition of her system. This destruction commences when, as she believes (whether or not it is correct is immaterial), she was weaned, at the age of five. She feels as if she had been thrown out of the garden of Eden. Is it not understandable that she rebels with all her might? She suddenly feels herself forced to call God and her parents bad names. The fact that she does not know why she does it protects her and permits her to continue it. Her procedure is a distinct act of revenge. Given a similar set of circumstances, we can produce the same reaction in every child. She behaves intelligently throughout. The guilt lies with those persons who prepared for her a paradise of pampering and permitted her to remain too long a time in it.

I was furious with those whom I liked best.

As we now know, they are the ones to blame.

It was as if the devil had whispered it into my ear. The harder I tried to restrain myself, the more violently I swore.

This is a mechanism which every patient produces. Our answer is: then don't try to restrain yourself. Let us see what happens psychically. Exactly this: my thoughts are so strong and I am innocent. Here lies the complete justification of the neurotic who

ADOLESCENT DIFFICULTIES

complains that he feels forced to perform certain acts (compulsion neurosis). Why does she have to do this? Because she has no other means. She would rather force her mother to continue to nurse her, but her mother refuses. She could easily force her father, if he could assume the rôle of wet-nurse. *But I wanted to become healthy*, says the patient. The wish is the proof that she is sick; we therefore advise renouncing the wish. Individual psychologists are skeptical about wishes, in contradistinction to other psychologists. As long as somebody wishes he is sure that nothing will happen. The assumption that volition precedes a deed is contradictory to psychology in general. When we hear of wanting, we may convince ourselves that nothing is going to happen. On the other hand, when something happens, we hear nothing of a wish.

My face often became deeply flushed from the effort I made to repress my thoughts, but the thoughts did not vanish. In order to apologize to myself, I said, "The boarder is a dog, not father."

Cultivation of compulsory thoughts—useless puttering.

CHAPTER III

THE DEVELOPMENT OF A NEUROSIS

NEUROTIC cases resemble one another to a certain extent. The burden of a neurosis is always the same: anxiety in anticipation of a defeat in communal life. As a result of such anxiety, the neurosis appears in the exonerating form of an illness which detaches all responsibility from the "sufferer" and which is, in reality, nothing more nor less than an effective flight from the expected danger. To give in other words a picture corresponding to the viewpoint of a neurotic: the neurotic views life as a battle in which his own life is constantly in danger (the lives of others being unimportant to him). The nearer he comes to the battle front, which is life, the greater is his nervousness and apprehension concerning his own safety. Finally his anxiety overcomes him and he takes to his heels or attempts to insure a certain measure of safety for himself by burying himself in trenches lying as far from life's battle-front as possible.

The form a person chooses for his neurosis depends upon his behavior pattern and fictive goal. However,

THE DEVELOPMENT OF A NEUROSIS

even the various forms of neuroses do not differ very much from each other, and persons completely unlike in type, but having the same sort of neurosis, frequently choose the same form for the neurotic manifestation. This is true especially of compulsion neuroses. It seems as if mankind were not able to create many variations.

Nevertheless I suffered from deep remorse. I looked at my parents and thought, "If you knew what abusive remarks I make about you!"

Any one not knowing the teachings of individual psychology might conclude from such a remark that the girl pities her parents. Her conscience pricks her because of her wretched behavior. Speaking of remorse reminds us of an error in the Freudian school of psychoanalysis: The Freudians lay great stress upon the feeling of guilt. But they misunderstand it. The feeling of guilt is an inferiority feeling in disguise. It makes itself apparent when some one breaks the laws of social life and it indicates at the same time that the lawbreaker recognizes these social laws as intrinsically right. Nevertheless there is in the feeling of guilt neither the intention nor any other indication that the delinquent will thereafter obey the laws; that is to say, that he will make his life conform to or harmonize with social life. Indeed, we believe that what Nietzsche says is true—remorse is indecent. If

THE CASE OF MISS R.

remorse really meant what naïve philosophers assume, the feeling would be followed by a change in behavior. Such a feeling, however, is usually the continuation of a useless activity (always remembering that remorse as here used is in connection with a neurosis).

On that account we permit ourselves to interpret the girl's statement otherwise. We have seen that this girl wanted to be the center of attention. Her constant desire is to be first. We do not believe that she has given up this desire. She now feels herself superior, for when she says, *If you knew what things I say about you,* it means, "I am more than you. You are blind. You understand nothing," and saying *Father is a dog* means, "I am better than father." Thus we can see more clearly how the girl attempts to elevate herself above others. When she feels remorse, the fact is not altered; on the contrary, the remorse proves that she has endeavored to obey the tendency to degrade her parents. We find the tendency to degrade others only in those people who feel inferior. An individual can compensate for his feeling of inferiority by elevating himself over others, or by degrading others. In either case he has gained a certain height over them. That is to say, one can create this distance by elevating oneself or lowering the others. The degradation of others and elevation of oneself are not in the least diminished by a dis-

THE DEVELOPMENT OF A NEUROSIS

quieting conscience. Quite the reverse, for such a person is then given an additional excuse to pity himself, or to elevate himself still more.

Some neurotics feel impelled to demonstrate their superiority to their fellow men. Others are satisfied if their neurotic striving creates a mood which permits them merely to feel superior.

I wanted to escape these thoughts, but they seized me over and over again.

They even disturbed me when I prayed at night; then I had to repeat my prayer. It was horrible.

This hammering, this underlining, this absolutely useless emphasis in description are part of the nature of a neurosis; that is, to make something out of nothing. It brings the neurotic nearer his goal of godlikeness.

It stopped only when I went to school.

We observe quite often that school life is able to change conditions. The situation has probably become more favorable. She is no longer confronted as seriously with the problem: am I more than father or not? Perhaps her father has commenced to spoil her a little more again.

I suffered from sleeplessness very early in life, at the age of six or seven.

THE CASE OF MISS R.

Reading a sentence like the foregoing reminds us of our experiences. It is obvious that sleeplessness will not remain unnoticed, that a relation to the environment is present. If the child cannot sleep, father and mother are directly involved and participate in a poor night. Disturbances during the night are the customary methods of those children who want to have some special attention at night. It makes no difference whether they make trouble going to bed or falling asleep, whether they sleep poorly, suffer from pavor nocturnus (fear of the night) or bed-wetting, whether they talk in their sleep or walk in their sleep. It always means: one has to take care of me. The night is used to busy the persons around her.

It was very hard for me to fall asleep, and in the morning I was the first to awaken.

It is true that the night, and with it sleep, are the greatest enemies of all spoiled children. Nervous adults are also furious when others sleep. In many neuroses this disturbance is markedly in the foreground.

At this point it might be well to insert a few observations on nervous insomnia in general. Sleeping, just as well as eating, is seemingly of far greater importance than it really is. Certainly we need sleep in order to renew ourselves. But sleeping is something

THE DEVELOPMENT OF A NEUROSIS

like breathing; nature usually compels us to take the amount we need.

Nervous sleeplessness, like all nervous symptoms, serves different purposes. It may be a vital connecting link in the chain of a nervous life system. We have frequently seen that a nervous person thinks constantly of how he can make himself superior. Sleep is generally considered of extreme importance. The inability to sleep can be used as an effective protest against the environment. It usually affords a means to penalize or complain of certain members of one's household. If a patient complains of sleeplessness during psychotherapeutic treatment, he holds the doctor responsible for it as if he would thereby indicate to him the uselessness of his therapeutic efforts. Or the sleeplessness will be used to prove illness as soon as that shows itelf the most effective way to the establishment of superiority, and of one's own will. This will is usually directed toward finding a good alibi, so as to be able to plead inability to work or to face a problem, and likewise to make rules for others —I am nervous, can't sleep, so every one in the house must be quiet; doors must be closed gently; voices must be lowered; every one must be home early, and so on.

The sufferer from sleeplessness emphasizes his symptoms so strongly that it can be inferred he demands recognition of his difficult situation. When

THE CASE OF MISS R.

this recognition is given him, he is freed from all responsibility for whatever blunders he may make in life, and as a further consequence, will value twice as much whatever success he may have, since he has been successful in spite of his handicap. The neurotic realizes the expediency of this method from his own experience or from having seen the effect of another's illness on the environment and on himself. So long as the psychic significance of the situation has not been understood, we are not surprised when the doctor, or whatever remedies may have been tried, obtain for the patient only a confirmation of his alleged illness.

It is thus evident that nervous sleeplessness is arranged to serve as shield and weapon for the protection of the threatened self-esteem. Nervous people who choose the symptom of sleeplessness generally have other characteristic indications of the nervous character. Most of them are very ambitious, but lack confidence in their ability to attain their end. They place too great value on success and exaggerate the difficulties of life; they are cowardly and afraid to make decisions and they love to rule. The thoughts of such a patient during the time when he should be dozing off, are either a means to keep him awake, or they contain the kernel of the psychic difficulty on account of which the sleeplessness has been provoked.

What the patient wants to construct is a broad

THE DEVELOPMENT OF A NEUROSIS

chasm between himself and his pernicious, neurotically unattainable goal, which will absolve him of failure and give him a good excuse to cease struggling. The symptom disappears as soon as the patient realizes that his inability to sleep is a means by which he can avoid the responsibility for the solution of those problems with which life burdens all mankind. When he ceases to look upon his sleeplessness as an inexplicable fate, he is forced to abandon this symptom.

My father was so exercised about my poor sleep that he himself could not sleep any more.

The confirmation follows on the heels of our interpretation.

Then I pretended to be asleep, and when father stole into the room on tiptoes, I breathed slowly and deeply as if I were sleeping.

This sounds loving and considerate. The child, of course, has a certain feeling of tenderness for her father; she sometimes gives in when she thinks she has gone too far. However, this girl has every reason to feel quieted as she notices her father's apprehensiveness. After seeing her father prowling in the dark and then not sleeping for the rest of the night, she may have made the compromise: since I have gone so far as to force father out of bed, I am satisfied.

On our floor lived another tailor who had many

THE CASE OF MISS R.

*children, four girls and two boys. One of the boys,
Poldi, was my age; I played with him. He was a little
roughneck, dirty and barefooted. I imitated him.*

This looks innocent and harmless, imitating a boy.
However, if we had an opportunity to uncover more
of what went on in her mind, we should doubtless
find a wish to change into a boy. It is the small re-
mainder of a great, general trait: it is the protest
against being a woman in a world where men are
generally considered superior; where they have the
more advantageous positions, greater freedom and
apparently greater physical strength. I have termed
this manifestation the masculine protest.

Our studies have shown us that the masculine protest assumes a central position in every neurosis. It
proceeds from the child's feeling of weakness in comparison to the grown-ups. Out of this grow a feeling
of dependence and a longing for tenderness, a
physiological and psychological dependency and subordination. It is, in a word, a branch of the general
struggle for supremacy which springs from the feeling of inferiority. As the name, masculine protest,
implies, it contains a special connotation.

Because of his intense longing for security, the
nervous person is inclined to divide the world into
contrasting parts, to live only according to extremes
and to treat his problems in the same way—all or
nothing, victory or defeat, up above or down below,

40

THE DEVELOPMENT OF A NEUROSIS

and so on. The many steps in between might prove perplexing and so they are dispensed with.

Two such extremes are to be found in the phrase masculine-feminine. From careless or tactless remarks made by adults, and from its own unprejudiced observation of the world in which it grows up, a child speedily learns that in our civilization men are considered superior to women. The rôle of a man seems generally to be more advantageous and better suited to help oneself out of the feeling of inferiority. The wish thereupon develops, "I want to be a man." A boy can fulfill this wish in his behavior. That is to say, aside from the fact that he is physically a male, he can act according to his idea of how a man should conduct himself. A girl cannot do this.

For a boy, however, the wish, "I want to be a man," has a somewhat different meaning than for a girl. He feels obliged to fulfill the ideal of man which our culture has set; whereas the masculine protest in a girl does not express anything but the wish to enjoy the advantages and privileges accorded men.

When there is already a disposition to nervous disturbance in the life of a child because of an aggravated feeling of inferiority, the child—no matter whether boy or girl—will interpret this man-woman conception as antagonistic extremes and purposively exaggerate this interpretation. The child will attach to the word "man" all that means superiority (in its

41

THE CASE OF MISS R.

own belief), and will associate with the word "woman" everything that points to inferiority. Its own feeling of inferiority is sensed as strongly feminine (as one sees the actual sex has nothing to do with the interpretation), and a desperate attempt is made to compensate for the imagined deficiency by assuming masculine characteristics. That is the verbal diagram of the masculine protest.

In the strict apperceptive scheme of the neurotic, all those qualities which are termed passive are stamped as feminine, such as docility, mildness, kindness, subordination, cowardice, patience, etc.; while active character traits such as aggressiveness, stubbornness, obstinacy, impudence, insubordination and the desire for power and freedom, are accepted as masculine. The goal is to rule, to be superior. Where it seems impossible to reach this goal by direct aggression, the nervous person chooses the variation of "a masculine protest with feminine means"; that is to say, he tries to attain the dominating state of masculinity through a display of weakness, exaggerated tractability, or through the arrangement of sickness.

We can therefore conclude that this girl's wish, always to be the first, is not in accord with the unhesitating acceptance of the feminine rôle. *Wouldn't it be easier if I were a boy?*

There was a big heap of sand in the courtyard.

THE DEVELOPMENT OF A NEUROSIS

There we played grocers. The sand represented the victuals.

She describes their games. At this point I want to make a few remarks on the significance of children's games. Groos points out very clearly in his book, "The Plays of Children," what we must not understand by playing. I cannot comprehend how any one can speak of a play instinct after reading this book.

The so-called play instinct is nothing other than the attempt by the child to prepare itself for the future by making use of the limited means at its disposal. The child trains itself for the rôle of an adult by occupying itself with games which seem nothing more than playful to us. The imitation of grown-ups is very significant and obvious, and especially the imitation of those adults (or their conduct) who appear to the child worth while. The games are never senseless, but are always a step toward the future goal of the developing human being. It is all the same whether the child plays with a toy railroad or builds houses, or plays "husband and wife" or "Indian and princess." The child takes its play as seriously as an adult his work. Adults should therefore regard such games seriously and not interfere in an asinine, superior fashion. A child learns through play. Dostoievski once remarked that there is an artistic quality in the games of children. We individual psy-

THE CASE OF MISS R.

chologists understand this train of thought very well. Children have not the strength adults have with which to tackle a piece of work. Their greatest yearning, however, is to do as adults do. And so they use tricks in order to make believe they are grown up.

There was a dog in our house named Bello which belonged to a box manufacturer.

As a rule the relation between children and dogs is close, because dogs comply with the children's striving for recognition; they obey, they let themselves be mastered. Children who have a marked striving for recognition are strongly attracted by dogs. On the other hand, if all a child wants is to be watched continually by its mother, it may be afraid of dogs. The fear of dogs is then used to compel the mother always to be present. Such children are more discouraged than those who make friends with dogs. Nevertheless, as the example clearly shows, the two methods grow out of the same root, the feeling of inferiority. Only the varying intensity of the feeling calls forth different reactions.

This dog pulled a little carriage. It got lots of horsemeat sausages which lay by its hut. Poldi always wanted to steal one of the sausages, but the dog didn't like Poldi. One day Poldi crept carefully to the hut, grabbed a sausage and devoured it in an instant. That delighted me tremendously. I said to him,

THE DEVELOPMENT OF A NEUROSIS

"The sausage lay next to the dog's dirt and now you are eating it."

Again we see the tendency to degrade, *the sausage lay next to the dog's dirt.* The wish to elevate herself over others never leaves her.

He did not care. The box manufacturer had a large, covered wagon. He sometimes took us with him. We were always happy when we sat in the wagon.

She seems to like the company of boys.

Two old women lived on the second floor, and each of them kept several prostitutes. These prostitutes did not get up before noon or afternoon.

Children are often attracted when they see others wearing beautiful clothes. When their own circumstances are quite straitened, when they themselves have shabby clothes and are forced to suffer the bitterness and numerous discomforts of poverty, the contrast strikes them sharply. Limited by their childish judgment, they conclude that better clothes mean a better life, which they would also like to have. The purely social inferiority stings them and they seek a simple, quick and sure compensation. We can understand how some children are thus drawn to the road of misery, and we shall not be surprised to see these girls playfully prepare for the profession of a prostitute when they believe they can reach the goal of superiority in this direction.

THE CASE OF MISS R.

The prostitutes often threw money from their windows down to the street for which we were sent to buy them cigarettes and beer. Although I never saw more than the foyer of their apartment, I liked to be there. The furniture appeared very fashionable to me.

The prostitutes are not held in as much contempt by simple people as by the well-educated bourgeois, so we can see how the ranks of the prostitutes are always replenished.

I could watch them dress themselves from the hall window. I felt sorry for one of them who looked as if she were tubercular. But when she was dressed and had painted her face, she looked quite different than from the window. Some of the women were very vulgar and yelled through the house; it was a bedlam.

That is a distinct aversion. We do not presume she will ever go the way of prostitution.

I remember a few things about Lina. We subscribed for "The Book for Everybody." Lina read the serial in it and was eager to get the installment each week. She always asked for the periodical. Father did not like to have her read the novel and we agreed to conceal the magazine when it came. I, too, promised not to say anything. However, when Lina came into the room, I cried, "The magazine is here."

THE DEVELOPMENT OF A NEUROSIS

She could not obey; she rebelled.

One evening Lina copied a love letter from a book. Father and mother were in the kitchen; Lina was called out. I jumped out of bed, made a blot on the letter, went back to bed and pulled the blanket over my head.

Malice. She triumphs in that she knows something the others do not know. In addition, she feels powerful since she can obstruct her sister's plans, spoil her mood, and perhaps prevent her sister's making an important decision. The tricks and bad habits of children are always resorted to as a lever by which to raise themselves above others, the more powerful members of their environment. They damage, spoil or destroy almost always the property of others. Their hatred directs attention to the fact that they feel themselves so insignificant. One sees that they are distinct acts of revenge produced by a feeling of inadequacy.

When Lina saw the ink spot, she cried. After a while she went out of the room again and I repeated my nasty trick. She scolded me. I imitated her in every way. She was nine years older than I and she was like a second mother to me.

She can imagine a kind woman only in the form of her mother. That is characteristic of spoiled children.

THE CASE OF MISS R.

I tried hard to imitate Lina's handwriting. I liked her triangular flourishes. Father wanted me to write naturally.

There is no such thing as an imitative instinct. We imitate something because it pleases us, because it appears efficacious in our attempt to achieve superiority. Imitation, therefore, belongs in the realm of the striving for recognition and must be so understood. The imitation of her older sister indicates that the child imitates only that which fits into her style of life.

As a small child I would run up and down the steps in front of the church like one possessed. My mother had to drag me home with her by force.

This is perhaps pleasure in motion, or the child runs away so that the mother has to run after her.

Father was very religious; he taught me at an early age to make a cross when I passed a church and he gave me religious pictures. I began to collect religious pictures.

We believe that children collect things because it makes them feel strong. One can find collections which are absolutely senseless. The child collects in order to satisfy her striving for recognition.

I had a lot of pictures. In the evening I spread them in two rows under my pillow and on top I put a guardian angel. Otherwise I could not have fallen

48

THE DEVELOPMENT OF A NEUROSIS

asleep. I prayed until I was short of breath. I prayed for every one I liked, for my grandmother, uncles and aunts.

It is not difficult to train a child to such behavior. What does "I prayed for every one" mean? The fate of this person is in my hand. Such a child feels superior. This form of praying, so incompatible with reality, is often a symptom of a compulsion neurosis.

(A rich man had to support his three poor sisters and this annoyed him a great deal. He prayed to God that He might protect them and prevent them from being burnt to death. If he did not pray, he could not fall asleep for fear they might eventually be burned. Every day he rejoiced that they had not perished by fire. "I have their lives in my hand; I am responsible for their welfare.")

Christmas was a great event. Father sent me to the café "so that Santa Claus might in the meantime bring the presents."

CHAPTER IV

THE STYLE OF LIFE

A PSYCHOLOGIST may commence the study of a life story where he will; he will always find that the particular life he is investigating is directed toward a certain goal. In order to understand a person's life, it is necessary to discover the thread which runs through all his symptoms and which can be traced directly to his goal. We can also call this thread the style of life of a human being. The style of life is the special manner in which a human being faces life and answers the challenge of existence; how he feels, thinks, wants, acts; how he perceives and how he makes use of his perceptions. The style of life is formed by early childhood influences, developed in early childhood, and is guided by the goal of the person who follows it unquestioningly.

A gloomy mood prevailed at home. My parents had quarrelled again. I do not remember about what.

Children who are constantly the center of attraction, like this one, cannot bear having their parents quarrel. Not because they want peace, but because

THE STYLE OF LIFE

they feel excluded when the others are busy with each other. For that reason they frequently try to prevent quarrels in the family. The child does not remember what her parents quarrelled about; only that they did quarrel.

Father asked me to stay in my room and turn my face to the wall because Santa Claus was just passing the window. So I turned around. Lina took my hand. Then a bell rang and we went into the Christmas room.

It is interesting for the individual psychologist to consider whether or not children should be told such fairy tales. One must not be too cautious. Those who insist upon explaining everything in the light of sexual or other problems, miss the point. Children do not care very much whether these tales are true or not; they take them as a conventional nonsense, as a modus dicendi. I have never seen a child as excited at the discovery that Santa Claus does not exist as were those who were eager to explain the matter. We know that we tell our children too many fables; the question remains open how far one can go. However, this is not the main problem in the matter of bringing up children, at least not if one does not include with it the more serious tendency to restrict a child.

All restrictions not based on common sense have the effect of lessening the courage of a child and of mak-

THE CASE OF MISS R.

ing it believe that the reality of life is much more dangerous than it is. What results is an attempt to evade realities of life by resorting to neurotic alibis. Questions such as what fairy tales one should tell a child and up to what age, answer themselves according to the law of common sense. One must not forget that children are initially not as stupid as many adults have unfortunately become.

A large Christmas tree stood on the table with candles burning. In front of it I saw a big slate on a stand and, beside it, a doll. I think I also got a picture book. I rushed to my presents, admired them and immediately started to scribble on the slate with chalk. I could not write at that time.

Let us recall what we have said about the increasing interest in all visible things. Perhaps we shall find a verification. This scene, remembered for so many years, shows that the child paid a great deal of attention to visible objects, even if it turns out later that the details remembered are not true. The extremes of beauty and ugliness attracted this girl's notice.

Lina received a picture album and a red hat. I prepared a bed on the couch for my doll. Before falling asleep I got up and looked to see whether it lay comfortably.

THE STYLE OF LIFE

I looked confirms our assumption.

Next Christmas Milli, a friend of mine, advised me to surprise my parents and Lina with written greetings. I bought stationery used for this purpose, trimmed with gold and angels.

We perceive this girl's qualifications for the decorative arts. Asked for what profession she would be fitted, we should answer that she has trained in the direction of drawing. A vocational guidance advisor would have to keep this fact in mind. (Dressmaker or fashion sketcher.)

"Which profession would you advise?" is a question often put to psychologists. Many young people know very well what they would like to do; they have consciously or unconsciously prepared themselves for some occupation. The relatives like to assume that this is an instinctive choice. That is not right. The choice of a vocation arises out of childhood influences, sometimes influences felt in infancy, and the so-called instinct is a manifest training for the future calling.

We have to reckon with more difficulties in those cases where there is no predominant inclination and obviously no talent. First of all, it is highly probable that such people are much further away from and considerably more hostile to the question of work

THE CASE OF MISS R.

than those who have in some way prepared themselves. They have avoided coming to any decision on the problem of work, (one of the great social problems, as we know). They have shoved it aside for the time being as if it could be disposed of once and for all by such a manœuvre. These tactics remind us somewhat of the ostrich which sticks its head in the sand when in danger, in the belief that no one sees it because it can see no one. Such children are either deeply discouraged or they have been too comfortable to be bothered by the question of occupation, which comes to about the same thing.

In order to decide to what profession a young person is best suited, one must draw the necessary conclusions from his life story, his remembrances, the statements of various members of the family, and his own behavior. The sort of milieu from which he comes will be easily recognizable, and the milieu in which he fits can then be determined; to which sense type he belongs (visual, auditory, motor); what his general attitude toward life is; what he liked to do and what he really did as a young child; and so on. When a clear picture of the youth, of his character traits and compensatory strivings has been formed it is usually easy, with the help of our individual psychological experience, to find that occupation which best suits the pattern of this personality.

Milli had a little book full of Christmas wishes.

THE STYLE OF LIFE

She picked out three of the shortest for me and prepared to help me copy them.

This girl is capable of social contact.

Though she spelled every single word out for me, I spoiled a great many sheets. Again and again I had to run downstairs to fetch fresh paper. I exerted myself to the utmost and was glad when I finished my letter at last. It was crammed with mistakes, but my parents and Lina enjoyed it immensely.

You see how one is induced to help this child forward, how well she is liked. The girl is accustomed to being favored. We can predict that when she is finally faced with a difficult situation, she will react acutely; she will bear misfortune less bravely than her step-sister Lina. She is like a hot-house plant. When she is in a less sheltered position and is confronted with a situation where she has to give and cannot only take, she will break down.

As soon as I could write correctly, I composed long letters to Santa Claus, a whole list of things I wanted, written in a very affectionate manner.

Our assumption of the expectant attitude is confirmed. Her attitude in life is to expect things from others and to give as little in return as possible.

I imagined that Santa Claus descended from

THE CASE OF MISS R.

heaven on a long ladder placed at the end of the world, in order to buy presents in the Christmas shops. I pictured him in detail.

Visual type.

Corpus Christi day was almost as important a festival as Christmas Day. Father once gave a donation so that I could walk under a little canopy dressed up like a little angel.

A sense for festivities.

The night before that day I could hardly sleep.

The anxiety which precedes decisions or unusual events is increasing.

I was awake at about five o'clock and peeped through the window to see if the weather was good. When I heard the hammering which accompanied the fastening of the little trees and saw flowers spread over the walks, I was overjoyed. At half-past eight father brought me to the gathering place of the procession. I wore an angel costume with a crown and wings. Then I was placed under my little canopy and permitted to carry an image of the Holy Virgin.

These recollections show the girl's interest in external beauty.

We had to wait quite a while. It was pretty cool so father brought me hot tea from a neighboring cof-

56

THE STYLE OF LIFE

fee house. My wings, made from goose feathers, became so heavy that father had to take them off. Thus I trotted along, with a crown on my head, under the red canopy which was carried by four girls in white dresses. When we came near our house, I was too proud to look up to our windows. I imagined that I was almost an angel.

The child identifies herself with an angel to such an extent that she feels it humiliating to have to live in such a poor house.

Father followed along on the sidewalk, carrying the wings in his hand.

The girl's relation to her father signifies that she dominates him.

I liked to go to church and never omitted making the sign of the cross when I passed one. But when I passed a church in a trolley car or just happened to be with other girls who I knew would not make the cross, I was afraid to display my piety and fought with myself as to whether I should make the cross or not.

Children are naturally dependent upon the opinions of other and older persons. They learn from their parents the latter's interpretation of the world and must believe it until they can or want to think sufficiently for themselves to correct it. Mass sugges-

THE CASE OF MISS R.

tion also operates somewhat along this line. An individual in a mass no longer acts as he would act if he were quite alone; he falls back into a childlike state where he credulously accepts and follows the declarations of supposedly more experienced, more learned persons. In a mass each individual tries to make himself a part of a unified whole.

The conception of a "mass" implies that every one does not do what he wants, that he removes what disunites and aims at what unites. He who produces a slogan to which others are susceptible, creates unity. One has to consider mass suggestion. It is not true that an individual in a mass acts according to his own opinion; all the individuals form a stream which attempts to flow in one channel. And it becomes the supreme task of a mass to act homogeneously and without detailed investigation.

If I neglected to make the cross, I was conscience-stricken. I was afraid I should be punished by accidents.

She fights for that which is instilled in her by tradition; namely, the preservation of her individual personality. The conscience pangs are an attempt to fight off mass suggestion.

I was painfully exact with my confessions. I searched through father's old prayer books and wrote down a great many sins which I had never com-

THE STYLE OF LIFE

mitted, and then explored my memory for more sins.

We find that frequently. She wants to boast of many sins.

Then I asked father whether he knew a few more sins and if it was a sin to be troubled with flatulence. I had much trouble with the list of sins to be handed to the priest, which grew tremendously long. Since I was ashamed of having so many sins in front of the other children, I began to write such small, compressed letters that when I was in the confession chair, I could hardly decipher my own writing.

In reality such boasts tend to correct themselves. She boasts much, but she cannot make use of it.

At Easter, when I was in the fourth class, I partook of the Lord's Supper for the first time. I felt so peculiar that day, quite different from other days; so holy, I might say. I almost did not dare move around, because I had eaten of Christ. I thought my friend Olga unworthy because she had not taken it as seriously as I.

She wants to be in the ranks of the highest.

I enjoyed the tales from the Arabian Nights immensely. Father and Lina read them to me before I could read. When I heard the story of the merchant and the ghost, in which the merchant slays the ghost with a date pit, I asked father for some money and

THE CASE OF MISS R.

bought dates. Then I seated myself in a corner, threw pits into the air, and imagined that I had killed a lot of ghosts.

Such things happen when a child is about eight years old. A boy once thought that some one wanted to kill and devour him. Some people had made stupid remarks. The boy believed it still more when he was sent to a house to be "fed"; he thought that he would be put to death there.

I never liked to eat. . . .

Pampered, struggling child. The people around her lay much stress on eating. Where there is much stress laid upon cleanliness, a child becomes dirty; when the digestive function is overrated, difficulties in the choice of food or defecation arise. It is to be recommended that no overvaluation of natural functions ever become apparent to children.

I stimulated my appetite by the thought of fairy tales wherein sumptuous repasts were served. Or when I had to eat rice, for instance, I imagined a wicked witch who, in the shape of a beautiful woman, would eat only a few grains, but who secretly devoured corpses in the graves at night. In this way I consumed the rice grain by grain.

Notice how this girl identifies herself with every

THE STYLE OF LIFE

single figure in the fairy tales. She could eventually have become an actress.

When we had cutlet, I imagined—that was my own invention—that the fork was a woman and the morsel on it her hat; then I let the hat-morsel on the fork-woman walk around the plate several times and afterwards ate it.

These are the well-known tomfooleries of children. They always have to listen to, "Eat now; otherwise you won't grow up!" They see clearly of what importance it is to the adults that they (the children) eat well. A child that feels inferior or oppressed— and only such a child comes upon the idea of protesting—can hardly find a better way by which to manifest an apparent superiority than by not yielding to the demands and commands of the adults, or as here, to laugh at them. Especially when the protest appears so skilfully veiled, as in the play of this child with her food, the parents are quite powerless when they do not see through the trick. The child triumphs and proceeds to new strategies.

When I drank I often fancied that I was in a desert. All the others were dying of thirst and were sucking one another's blood. . . .

She speaks on several occasions of things which might be called cruel. Children are often cruel with-

THE CASE OF MISS R.

out thinking anything of it. Who has, as a child, never tormented an animal? Not for the sake of tormenting but out of pure curiosity. What will a fly do when I tear its wings off? How do the wings really look? It does not usually occur to children that they inflict pain upon the fly; they themselves don't feel any pain.

Where the cruelty is conscious and intended as such, it serves, as in the case of the masculine protest, as a means of achieving one's object by force or to give oneself the impression of peculiar power. A child may train itself to cruelty or barbarity in order to harden itself and thereby feel manly, or it uses this hard-heartedness as a bugbear, a threat or instrument for oppression, always, however, with the same goal of self-elevation at another's expense. Daydreams of savagery are either a mental preparation, a training, as it were, toward the deed, or a weak substitute for cowardice. This is not to be understood as praise of cruelty. Courageous people need no cruel fantasies.

Sometimes fantasies of cruel acts are connected with sexual excitement, but we believe it a blunder to generalize by concluding that cruelty has a sexual origin. Children in whom the fear emotion is connected with sexual emotion belong to a special type, but not every child is capable of producing a sex impulse by fear.

THE STYLE OF LIFE

I imagined I was the only one who had some water left. Then I thoroughly relished drinking a whole bottle sip by sip.

She fulfills the customary requirements of social life only under certain conditions.

In order to make my food taste better, I also liked to think that a famine had arisen and that I was the only one who still had provisions.

We should not be astonished to hear that the great flood had come and that she was the only human being saved. The legend of the great flood probably had its origin in a similar conceit.

I loved figs because they are mentioned in the Arabian Nights.

This is a fallacious causality. She deliberately makes something the cause and lets those consequences follow which serve her purpose; that is, to eat the figs.

I never liked potatoes.

We should not be surprised if she were to write, "because they are not spoken of in the Arabian Nights."

When we learned at school how potatoes had been discovered and how they had been wrongly prepared at first—it was not known then that only the roots were edible—I asked mother to boil a few for me

THE CASE OF MISS R.

and imagined that I had discovered them and nobody else knew how to prepare them.

Striving to be unique.

Mother made some sandwiches for me to take along to school; sometimes I had chocolate too. But I rarely touched my breakfast. I either gave my sandwiches away or took them home with me again. I felt a dislike for other children, for their hair, for their smell.

This is to be expected from this type of spoiled child. In the parks one often sees children who make gestures warding off the others. That means the exclusion of others. Such a gesture indicates a pampered child who abjures strangers and wants to be only with the familiar, yielding members of her family.

And I often wondered how they could eat anything in that smelly atmosphere.

Her superciliousness increases.

Following father's example, I acquired the habit of reading while I ate.

Such a remark from a girl who has never heard of individual psychology means much more than our sages are able to gather from it. She dislikes her feminine rôle. She imitates her father's manners with

THE STYLE OF LIFE

which she wishes to express that she would prefer to be a man like him.

I enjoyed most reading some fairy tale, such as, "Strong Hans," who has to eat through a mountain of delicious food for seven years. Even now my food tastes much better to me when I read with my meals.

In consideration of her ability to identify herself with another, we may say that she identifies herself with "Strong Hans." Again a boy.

Father told me one day that his former fiancée, Genevieve, had drunk her coffee without sugar. So I did the same. Mother took a lump of sugar in her mouth when she drank her coffee. I also imitated that.

She has not yet decided. She still hesitates. This will be a significant point in her development. She knows that she is a girl and cannot become a boy. Though in her remembrances there is a frequently expressed longing to be like a man, there is likewise evident a struggle to repress this longing, to reconcile herself to the feminine rôle and adjust herself to it.

My coffee had to be quite dark; milk horrified me.

This loathing of milk comes from the time when children commence to protest against the monotonous nourishment. All children are overfed with milk; they want to free themselves from a hated re-

THE CASE OF MISS R.

striction. The food given to children should be varied; they should not be fed with milk only.

If we were served with sweet, milky coffee at a children's party, I felt as if I wanted to vomit.

We hear a good deal about eating which permits the assumption of an organ inferiority of the digestive apparatus. Experience has taught us that those memories which are retained over a period of many years and remain particularly clear, frequently point to bodily deficiencies either acquired or congenital. In a former chapter we touched upon the fact that those remembrances are significantly clear which fit in with the individual's style of life and, on that account, permit the therapist to make certain deductions from them as to the style of life. But when we are told of remembrances which, directly or indirectly, recurringly call attention to a particular organ of the body, we can conclude that this organ either is not now or did not, at some former time, function normally. When recollections concern themselves principally with eating or food, they intimate a weakness of the digestive apparatus. Sometimes that can be factually proven; sometimes compensation started at a time when the young child could not yet form words and sentences by which to remember pictures or impressions; or the defect in the functioning was very slight and the compensation inaugurated

THE STYLE OF LIFE

by the body progressed so quickly and efficiently that only indirect associations remained in the memory. But they have always been difficulties, and the attempts to compensate for them have been impressed on the memory and can be traced back in the purposive remembrances of our patients.

My digestion gave me much trouble. I was constantly bothered with constipation. Most of all I hated enemas and suppositories.

Spoiled children frequently experience difficulties with the simplest functions.

Sometimes I sat on the toilet for an hour and could not defecate. And when there finally was some result, father used to be very glad. One day I was going to have an enema. Some friends of my parents were visiting us just then, among them a friend of father's, a pensioned captain. I simply refused to have the rubber tube inserted. Mother didn't know what to do. The captain, who knew everything better, came in and said to my mother, "You aren't managing that well; you have to do it this way," . . . *and all of a sudden the rubber tube slipped and the water went right into his face.* . . . *Once in a while I found red spots in mother's bed or on her nightshirt.*

Interest in what is visible.

When I asked her, "Mama, why do you bleed from

67

THE CASE OF MISS R.

your back?" she replied that she had piles from which she actually suffered at times. Then I crept to the seat where mother had sat and sniffed around it. Very soon I knew this smell so well that I could detect it on every woman.

A good sense of smell may signify an organ inferiority, but it would be a mistake to assume that only the under-functioning of an organ indicates a defect. Overfunctioning is just as much an inferiority and can give rise to exactly the same difficulties as when the organ operates badly. Normal functioning means neither too much nor too little. A hyperfunctioning of the sense of smell would, in our present culture, certainly lead to the same disastrous results as four hands instead of two hands and two feet.

I also tried to smell my own body so hard that I often got a headache from it. My main pleasure was to rub patches of silk against each other till they were hot and gave forth a peculiar odor. I sometimes called my friend Olga over to help me with this. We would sit down somewhere in a corner, rubbing and sniffing.

Pronounced faculty for smelling. The same tendency which she has in regard to investigating spiritual matters.

THE STYLE OF LIFE

I went to the theatre for the first time when I was four to see "Puss in Boots." The other children roared with laughter. I sat there and looked and listened with a serious expression. My parents asked me whether I liked it or not. Apparently they would rather have seen me laugh just as loudly as the others. They seemed disappointed because I did not move a muscle of my face and gave no sign of pleasure or displeasure.

The future grande dame!

Their inquisitiveness annoyed me. On the way home they insisted upon my telling them why I had looked on as morosely as if I were seeing a tragedy. I did not answer. The next day, however, I recited the contents of the entire play. They were all startled. Only then did they realize what a deep impression the play had made on me.

We have said that this girl may be on her way to becoming an actress. The play made an ineradicable impression on her.

A poor, Swedish baron came to our house. He had been compelled to leave his country on account of a duel in which he had killed his adversary. He had become the operator of a moving picture projector in a theatre. Once a week he invited us to the movies. We waited for him after the performance and then had supper together. Father ordered veal cutlet with

THE CASE OF MISS R.

fried potatoes and red wine. In a restaurant I could eat with great appetite.

The fussiest people consume everything in a restaurant. Our supposition is correct. Trouble while eating springs from the wish to make trouble.

Every week I looked forward with pleasure to that evening.

We could have foreseen that this child would be interested in the cinema.

When the baron received money from his people, he would treat all of us. Everybody drank a great deal of wine and the whole party was drunk. Only I remained sober which made me feel so lonely that I cried.

Every one was occupied with his happiness but not with her.

Later we used to visit frequently a restaurant in a building in which there was also vaudeville. We always sat in the dining room. I could not stand it there very long so I stole away by myself to the vaudeville show, stood beside the band and listened. When the waiters drove me away, I went out through one door and came in again through another. And if there was no chance of getting in, I peeped through a crack in the door. During the intermissions I would sneak in and take one of the empty seats.

THE STYLE OF LIFE

I should like to put in a word about children's visiting such performances. When I was two years old, my parents took me to hear some singers of popular songs. I heard good and bad things. I saw some operettas at the age of five or six. Who knows what might have become of me if they had not taken me along? I hope my power of resistance is appreciated since I had to swim through such turbid waters. These things are not so harmful as they seem; the anxiety of parents is exaggerated. One should not take children to horrifying performances. Social courage should be maintained and strengthened. But it is not justifiable to prohibit their seeing a funny piece. . . . One of my oldest remembrances is this: my parents had to go away and leave me and my older brother in the care of our governess. When my father returned, he was greeted by a strange sight. I was standing on the table, roaring out a popular song dealing with a woman who was anguished by the sight of a slaughtered chicken; she even emphasized the fact that her heart was bleeding. The chorus of this song, however, told how this woman, in spite of her pity for slaughtered animals, threw pots at her poor husband. I conclude from this childhood remembrance an early interest in finding out how even contradictions can be united in one pattern.

I found great pleasure in the performances. My

71

THE CASE OF MISS R.

cheeks burned. I listened attentively to every word. But I could not stand comedians.

We should not be surprised if she became a movie actress.

I always loved animals.

That is a common trait among children who want to rule. There is hardly anything in the world more obedient than a dog or a rabbit. Even such children who avoid social contact because they feel their superiority endangered can be gentle to animals. One should not deny children an acquaintance with animals. The real motive of this preference, however, is the feeling of superiority.

I never tormented them. Once only I cut a bedbug in half. Then I ran to my father to ask him whether it was a sin.

She wants to be the most pious of all.

I had a little rabbit. I trained him so that he hopped over to me when I called him. Once he bit me. I spanked him a little and decided not to look at him for the whole day.

Cruel punishment.

But no sooner had I taken him off my lap then I called him back, pardoned and kissed him and cried

THE STYLE OF LIFE

to think that he had forgotten himself so far as to bite me.

Feeling of grandeur.

I liked to play with his little tail, or I sat down with him on the couch, played the piano with his paws and sang a song.

What rabbits are good for!

No one else was allowed to come near him. I loved to scratch his nose softly with two fingers. He kept quite still. It seemed to do him good. After a while I had scratched off all the hair around his nose.

If in complicated cases a question arises as to how it can happen that some one gets the idea to rule by fear, the answer is that the person does not have the idea consciously, but he acts accordingly. He has, at some time or other, observed and retained a strong, unconscious impression of the observation that it is possible to rule by fear. In much the same fashion the girl finds out accidentally that one must scratch rabbits on the nose in order to please them and make them obedient. The origin of nervous symptoms is just as little miraculous as her discovery.

I was presented with an American dance-mouse by our boarder.

THE CASE OF MISS R.

Fond of animals.

Later on the boarder gave me a hedgehog which spread its quills when I came near it. I thought: that animal is nasty, it only stings me. I don't like it.

All animals are not obedient.

One day a little bird flew in through our window. It was a canary and it had a sore foot. We bought a cage for her and took care of her. Then she laid an egg and sat on it, a phenomenon quite puzzling to me. I was greatly delighted with the tiny, bare little bird. But the old bird let the young one die of hunger. I put the little corpse into a box and the box under the couch. When it started to smell, I buried it in the courtyard.

She makes a pompous ceremony of everything.

I was immensely fond of lady-birds. When I found one, I took a box, pierced some holes through it, covered the bottom with cotton, put a fresh leaf over it and put the lady-bird carefully on top of the leaf. I could play with it for hours and hours. And when it flew away I began to cry and nobody could console me.

This girl searches for a way in which she can feel her superiority to the full.

CHAPTER V

THE JEALOUSY MANIA

OUR boarder used to accompany us when we went on an outing. One day he stayed at home. Mother was quite angry; father noticed it immediately. On our way to the trolley station they began to quarrel.

At an early age this girl is made aware of jealousy in the family. She feels that her father is not satisfied when her mother is interested in other men. Jealousy is a lack of self-confidence and represents an attempt to win power over the person of whom one is jealous. The victim of jealousy never realizes that by resorting to such means he establishes at best only a semblance of power and, more frequently, exercises an intolerable tyranny which revenges itself upon the tyrant as surely as two and two make four. Jealousy is popularly looked upon as an instinctive feeling. To believe that a feeling as complicated as jealousy is inborn is an error. To accept such traits as inborn, inherited or instinctive characteristics relieves one of personal responsibility for consequences resulting from their manifestation. That is to say,

75

THE CASE OF MISS R.

such a stupid act can be much more readily justified when one can blame this character trait upon an inheritance. Otherwise one would have to assume full responsibility for what one has done. Severely neurotic cases of jealousy have shown us clearly that jealousy is nothing more than a combative mechanism to preserve one's prestige. It is combat assisted by feeling, and we reiterate: feelings are not arguments.

In consideration of the general prevalence of this disturbing trait I shall devote a few more words to the subject. A jealous person is always searching for proofs of his own influence and he experiments with every possible situation to prove this influence. The unappeasability with which a jealous person tests another person points clearly to his own lack of self-confidence, his minimum of self-esteem, and his insecurity. It is then easy to see how his jealous striving serves to thrust himself in the foreground, to attract attention to himself and to increase his value in his own eyes.

A jealous individual is always ready to believe that he has been thwarted or shoved to one side. Such an unfortunate reverts at once to his childish state of wanting everything. He makes the mistake of attempting to recover his superior position in relation to his partner. There are individuals who cannot bear having a fraction of attention withdrawn from them,

THE JEALOUSY MANIA

and who cannot suffer their partner's reading a book or newspaper in their presence. A glance, a conversation in company, a word of thanks for a courtesy, an expression of interest in another's picture, in a writer, or even in a relative, can lead, in serious cases, to violent outbursts of jealousy. It seems ridiculous for a wife to become indignant when her husband walks on ahead with another, or talks to some one else at a party instead of devoting himself exclusively to her. Such cases are frequent. Other people cannot tolerate their partner's praising another person. The customary remark is, "And how can you bother with such an idiot?"

In many cases it seems as if the unfortunate victim of jealousy can find no peace because he is not sufficiently secure personally to trust a peaceful happiness. Every possible chance is seized for new outbursts of jealousy designed to bind his partner more closely to him, to arouse pity, to punish the other, or to lay down rules. What is accepted as ordinary jealousy, is, in such cases, aggravated to the point where it becomes a severe neurosis, and finally passes over into what might be termed a jealous mania. It is to be noted that the principle is always the same, the sole distinction in various cases being quantitative.

Jealous rages are occasionally accompanied by hysterical weeping, nervous anxiety or depression, which all become transparent as soon as we observe the ef-

THE CASE OF MISS R.

fect. Or the jealousy is expressed in swearing, or a condemnation of the other sex in toto, which is an indication of the further progress of the effect of jealousy; namely, a preparation for the complete degradation of the opposite sex. Frequently pride prevents the conscious realization of jealousy, but the behavior remains the same.

In many cases again, jealousy is aggravated because the partner reacts to the helplessness of the jealous one with an unconscious self-sufficiency. The self-sufficient person in turn bases his feeling of superiority on the evident weakness of his jealous partner and, as a result, does not employ the right tone of voice or assume an attitude tactful enough to inhibit the growing feeling of jealousy in the other. Jealousy in connection with children leads often to the most serious pedagogical blunders. Such a generally prevalent character trait, and its developments, bring forcibly home to us how we poison our lives and our relations with others on the most trivial grounds, and how all this would be wholly unnecessary if we were willing to assume responsibility for our actions to a greater extent than we are taught to do to-day. To resume our story.

"You are annoyed because the boarder is not with us."

Here a marital fight seems to be commencing.

THE JEALOUSY MANIA

"Be quiet!"

It sounds like a modest request and most people who ask for nothing but quietness believe that they demand little. But they fail to realize that they, in fact, demand a great deal. Life means restlessness, disquietude. When I demand quietness, it means that I make laws for the behavior of others. It may sound modest, but it is a battle cry.

"Go and get him! Or stay home if you want to. You can live with him; I'm not going to stop you! If the child weren't alive, I'd have left you long ago."

We see the child standing in the midst of a matrimonial scene. She knows what it is all about. She receives impressions of married life. As you will remember, we found some traits in this girl which made us anxious about her future. There is no question that such scenes influence a child by giving her as graphic a picture of marriage as possible. It is very unfortunate that we become acquainted with the problem of marriage through the marriage of our parents. It is on this account that children frequently want to avoid marriage because it appears to them as a difficult problem; or they resolve to have a model marriage. Both resolutions lead them into innumerable hardships.

"What can you offer me? Not even a pair of stock-

THE CASE OF MISS R.

ings! You skinflint! What a life! You should have remained with your Genevieve!"

Genevieve had been an important person in the man's past life.

And they started yelling at each other.

I want to put this question to you: a pampered child is made an involuntary witness of a quarrel between her parents. She is accustomed to occupy the center of the stage. What does she do when she feels excluded? She must interfere.

I cried and tried to reconcile father and mother. The quarrel was horrible for me.

That sounds well-meant. We feel that it was horrible for her because she did not play a rôle in the argument, because she was a pure nobody.

Trembling all over (one cannot do enough in such a situation) *I entered the street car with them. Father made a sullen face; mother was furious.*

We can deduce from this scene alone that her father must have been a timid man. A tyrant does not act like that. Her mother was a woman who did not show herself in the least weak. She knew how to call her husband to account.

Mother wore a large straw hat which, according to the fashion in those days, sat pretty high on her head.

80

THE JEALOUSY MANIA

We were sitting in an open car and while the trolley was going fast, a wind came along suddenly and tore her hat off, carrying it out of the car. Father, still boiling with rage, jumped from the car in the wrong direction and fell down full length. Mother and I were terrified; the passengers sprang from their seats; the conductor signalled; the car stopped. Some people on the street helped father up and asked him whether he had hurt himself. He was deathly pale and could hardly answer. The conductor swore. Mother kept on saying, "My God, what do I care for that silly hat? How can you do such a thing?"

When some one is boiling with rage, he ought not to jump from a moving street car. It is easy to meet with an accident if one is preoccupied with something else. We are not trained to do more than one thing at a time; two are too many.

I knew very well that father would have not fallen headlong if he had not quarrelled. But I was glad that he escaped with only a few bruises.

Now comes a remark which can be understood solely by applying the individual psychological method.

The sensation we created was very painful to me. All the people looked at us.

In the light of our knowledge of the girl's per-

THE CASE OF MISS R.

sonality, we understand that she dislikes that kind of situation. That seems to contradict our statement that she is continually endeavoring to be the center of attention. She only wants to be the cynosure of all eyes, of course, when she is sure of making a favorable impression. Just as intensely as neurotics want to make a good impression, do they fear any situation in which they may appear to unfavorable advantage. One of the important problems of most neurotics is: how do I look? what do they think of me?

We can judge from the fact that this girl after so many years, remembers her feelings in the humiliating situation into which she believed she had fallen, how painful the emotion aroused by the general attention centered upon her must have been. But still, it was attention.

A policeman came along and wrote down father's name and address. When we were again seated in the trolley, I hooked my arm on his and did not leave his side again.

She is in the pleasant center again.

I was raving mad at the boarder. "Because of this damn fool," I exclaimed, "there are always quarrels. The devil take him!"

I imagine we have learned from former incidents in the history of this girl that, even in a state which

82

THE JEALOUSY MANIA

can be regarded as sane, she does not flinch from strong invectives. We shall not be surprised therefore, if she uses abusive language when she is in a severely neurotic state.

I never cared to go on outings with my parents from that time on. I was always afraid father would contrive to do something which could not be rectified.

We see that the disagreeable sensation and the fact that she was in the background had a prejudicial effect on her.

As far as I can think back in my life, my parents always quarrelled.

That is not quite correct, but since it is so strongly emphasized in her memory, we suspect that she will have difficulties in regard to her own future love relations. She will hesitate, retreat or try to escape. There is something to be said about escaping. We do not believe a neurosis to be a disease per se, but hold it to be a mistaken way of living. Therefore, in that which does not exist we cannot take refuge. I have no objection to using the terms illness or disease as figurative expressions, but the mechanism is different. One must never lose sight of the fact that a human being is not responsible for an infectious disease of which he is the innocent victim (diseases such as

THE CASE OF MISS R.

pneumonia, diphtheria, typhoid, etc.), but he is responsible for a neurosis. Disease is accompanied by damage to parts or to the whole of the organism; neurosis in itself is not. When certain organs become ill or are kept in a sickly condition by means of a neurosis, they were either defective or ill before. But such defects have nothing to do with the neurosis as such. There are definite relations between bodily illnesses and neuroses, but that does not make a neurosis an illness in itself.

This girl does not know anything of a disease; she is constructing, arranging, building up her life, and when something interferes with her normal progress, such an interference is called a disease. This conception, however, is far from her thoughts, even when they are compulsory thoughts. She knows quite well the difference between physical illness and these thoughts. The error consists in stating definitively that health lies on the one side and disease on the other.

A constant source of trouble was that father, in order to have mother free for his work, always wanted my sister to take me for a walk. She, however, preferred to read novels. She was a real bookworm and sometimes even read by the light of the moon. When mother cooked Lina's favorite dish, father became angry and said, "You are quite crazy about your Lina."

THE JEALOUSY MANIA

Discord is introduced between the two children. It is not remarkable that both girls feel neglected. The fact that this girl (the writer) is attached to her father justifies the assumption that her mother has not played her rôle very well. For some reason or other her mother did not succeed in holding this girl and the child is in the second phase. A critical attitude toward her mother has set in. It is sometimes difficult to find out just when such an attitude is first assumed. I, myself, liked my father more than my mother because he pampered me more. I did not then understand why. I certainly esteemed my mother very highly as a human being, and yet I withdrew from her. When I thought about it, I came to the following conclusion: When I was three years old, a younger brother of mine died. On the day of the funeral I was brought to my grandfather. My mother came to call for me there; she was crying bitterly. My grandfather consoled her and I noticed that she smiled. I could not forgive her this smile for many years; how can a mother smile on the day she buries her child? Later on I understood it better: my grandfather probably held out hope of future children to her. On the other hand, I might have thought: how glad I am that she can smile on such a sad day. I was very critical of her. Another remembrance: an uncle of mine asked me, "Why are you so harsh to your mother?" This shows how critical my attitude was

THE CASE OF MISS R.

toward her. Reconstructing the past, I can now see it myself. I was pampered by my mother during the first two years of my life because I was a sick child. I became accustomed to this pampering. A new child was born—that incident plays the same rôle in my remembrances that arabesques do in a piece of architecture—I was dethroned. My mother could no longer give me so much attention since she had to take care of the newborn infant. I could not forgive her for that. Then, in the second phase, my father took my mother's place which was what I wanted.

The girl's father is also angry because the mother cares so much for his stepdaughter.

One day, in a rage, father flung a dish of noodles on the floor. Mother often had secrets with my sister. Father could not stand it. When anger made him lose control of himself, he would begin to grind his teeth, throw the dishes on the floor, tear his underwear, trample his hat under foot and threaten to commit suicide. Once in a while we heard him say, "If I only had a revolver!"

We already know that this man is inclined to be jealous. That seems plausible when the memory of his wife's first husband comes up, caused by observing her prefer her older daughter. We would know how to cure this man; we would have to show him that he cannot bear being supplanted. We understand that

86

THE JEALOUSY MANIA

he feels helpless; only the helpless resort to such drastic means. This clamor for a revolver is typical; it is a threat frequently made.

Then he would run away, even leaving his meals untouched. I was crazy about father, was beside myself when this happened, and was in terrible anxiety about him. When they quarrelled, I always cried, begged him to be quiet and held his hand. That soothed him a little, but he would run away in spite of it. I waited apprehensively for his return, and when it took too long, I put on my hat and went along the street to the café to look for him. I usually found him there and we embraced each other as heartily as if we had not seen each other for years.

We recognize clearly from the above description that this child was a spectator of domestic troubles and that the problems of her parents' marriage disturbed her childish beliefs to her complete confusion.

CHAPTER VI

SEXUAL DEVELOPMENT

L ET us survey the story of this girl through the magnifying glass of individual psychology, in order to disclose all the connecting links which make this life a single chain. Let us review the story as historians or as artists who study the development of a work of art. We want to examine how a fact, an experience, a reaction, fits in with the other parts in order to find the general thread, or, as we may call it, the style of life.

Here is a spoiled girl, who is peculiarly attached to her father, who gets what she wants whenever she expresses a wish, and in whose future, for that very reason, we may anticipate great difficulties. When a pampered child leaves the home in which she has occupied a favorable position, she has not been trained to withstand hardship. And since she has some sort of presentiment of what lies in wait for her, she will try to preserve the old relations as long as possible, will be afraid of decisions and will approach her problems as slowly as she can. Her entire style of life appears then to have had a brake applied

SEXUAL DEVELOPMENT

to it. The hesitating attitude, as I have termed this general characteristic, is typical for every neurosis. The neurotic is always busy preparing to do something; sometimes very busy indeed. But before he puts one foot forward, objections are audible. He makes what looks like a start, but stops in time to prevent anything happening. He says "yes" which is supposed to express his readiness and willingness, but right on the heels of "yes" comes "but." And he remains in the same spot. Yes-but concretizes the typical attitude of all those persons who are nervous—possibly the most succinct expression we can find to define a neurosis.

It may be remarked that we often compare the character traits which the life story of this girl reveals with the peculiar characteristics of neurotics, so that we seem to intimate that her character appears neurotic to us. The objection may be raised that the girl has developed no neurotic symptoms and as long as that is not the case, a speculation as to her neurosis would be premature. As you will remember, however, we emphasized strongly, at the beginning of the story, the necessity of using our collective store of psychological experience and knowledge, and this experience includes not only the picture of the fully developed neurosis, but embraces as well an individual's preparation for a neurosis. Determining indications point to such a preparation and turn up

THE CASE OF MISS R.

regularly again and again in the early life of almost every neurotic. When we look back in a life story and see the appearance and reappearance of these preparatory traits, we can draw the empirical conclusion, without knowing in advance the rest of the story, that the life of the person concerned will degenerate into a neurosis at the first suitable opportunity. We, likewise must prepare ourselves for the eventual outbreak of the neurosis of this girl, in order not to overlook anything essential, or to lose the thread of her story. On this account the examination of even minute details may be of importance.

In this biography many apparently irrelevant details are mentioned—social relations and contact with persons who affect her life but slightly. In learning to understand her life, we are not so much concerned with that which is exciting in her experiences, but with that which has attracted her. All the little incidents must be taken into consideration to gain a complete picture.

Father was often sad. The reason for that was my unusual bodily weakness.

We see how much she is influenced by the fact that her father is anxious about her and that his life is devoted to her.

And when he was in good humor for several days, a reaction would immediately follow.

SEXUAL DEVELOPMENT

We recall that she was this man's only child.

He used to sit in his accustomed place without saying a word and with a sad face; one leg outstretched, the other bent and drawn under. Or he would sit on the table with his legs doubled under him, sewing and sewing, and if you spoke to him, he answered absent-mindedly. That always annoyed mother and so there was another quarrel.

It is to be borne in mind that this girl was deeply impressed by her father's position in relation to her.

During an exasperating quarrel father hit the glass door with his fist and hurt his hand very badly.

The attitude of her father to her mother, so different from his attitude to his child, became apparent to the girl and she felt herself superior to her mother.

He couldn't work for several weeks and had to visit the doctor every day. At that time he went out with me a good deal. I felt ashamed of being alone with him; I wanted mother to be there too.

That is an interesting remark. It is clear that the child had a feeling of guilt toward her mother. She was successful in supplanting her mother, therefore the feeling of guilt. We have seen how this girl wishes to be superior under any circumstances, superior even to her mother. There can be no doubt that a feeling

THE CASE OF MISS R.

of guilt can spring from such an attitude, that the girl fights for her mother's position only because of a lust for power. Other writers may say that such a feeling of guilt can only come from an Œdipus complex * because this girl, to express it mildly, has a libidinous inclination to her father. To such writers one must rejoin that there are other authorities who state that there are girls who have no Œdipus complex. This is the point at which he who does not fully apprehend the significance of the struggle for power may think that the girl wanted something which she was too frightened to take. In reality, however, she wants nothing but the dominating position in the family, and she has it.

When mother gossipped with a neighbor, father was beside himself. He was jealous of every one, but most jealous of the boarder who really did have an eye on mother.

We do not know how old the child was when she received these impressions. She is confused about time. When she was a small child she kept a sharp eye upon everything that went on about her. The position assumed by each one in the family grew clear to her. When a human being lives in the midst of active social relations, that is a way by which he can learn to understand human nature. No one who has been

* See page 145

SEXUAL DEVELOPMENT

carefully sheltered, before whom nothing was allowed to be said, can ever acquire such a fine psychological perception. The more children are allowed to observe all that goes on in their home, the better will be their psychological understanding. The pedagogues say, however, that certain disagreements and taut situations should not be allowed to develop in the presence of children. We do not claim infallibility for our recipe. Individual psychology is in a good position. It does not matter what happens in the environment. What does matter is that the child attaches itself to its surroundings, that it develops social feeling, and then difficulties cannot produce negative results.

Acquiring information touching upon sex is looked upon as one of the great dangers for children. This is a matter which exposes the thoughtless inconsistency of the sexual exponents. They say that the child is led astray by its school friends. This misleading is usually harmless and straightens itself out later, or the child simply does not believe what it has been told. In addition, one only learns what one is ready to learn. When serious consequences follow such an explanation, the blame is to be laid on the unintelligent rearing which prepared the ground for the production of unpleasant results. There are many "ugly" things besides sex.

It should not be taken for granted that children

THE CASE OF MISS R.

believe everything which is told them. When we were children, did we believe everything? When I was small, a boy told me that a butcher slaughtered human beings and sold the flesh. I didn't believe him. It is the same with a proffered explanation of sex. There is sometimes the greatest doubt of what is true. Children must be taught the truth with great care, so that they can have a firm hold on the useful side of life.

We once went walking and father started to quarrel with mother about the boarder, then raised his cane and threatened her, thereby accidentally striking me on the forehead. A swelling the size of a nut resulted. Father then controlled himself, but was most perplexed. I was so angry at the boarder that I said to father, "Come, father, let us go and leave mother behind."

The child's pugnacity is obvious. She uses everything to gain a victory over her mother.

Mother's position was not a favorable one. She was a pretty, cheerful woman and father killed her cheerfulness. He wanted to keep her in the house to take care of the home and to sew for him.

We may be positive that the deciding of this fact was not without harm to the child. It is certain that this child will begin to dread the fate of her mother.

SEXUAL DEVELOPMENT

She fears that such a fate can change the course of one's entire existence, and that the same thing may happen to her that happened to her mother. In this way she nourishes her suspicions about the dangers of love and marriage. She will never be trustful; she will watch to see if there are no indications that she also will be imprisoned in this fashion. She will be on her guard and learn to evade such problems.

One evening father brought home a pearl-handled revolver from the neighboring café. Mother and I recalled his frequent threats of suicide and had no peace until he returned the revolver to the owner of the café. I always shivered when a quarrel began, and they were almost always quarrelling.

The child's trepidation during her parents' disagreements is not as simple as she implies. There is always the possibility that she will become of no importance. Two persons occupy themselves without giving her any consideration. A child's interjection into its parents' quarrels is often due to the fact that it cannot endure being overlooked.

In spite of everything, however, I idolized my parents and watched over them jealously. Once when I noticed that my father started to follow a girl, I clung to his arm and cried, "You aren't going to follow that monkey-face!"

THE CASE OF MISS R.

That is not to be wondered at. It appears to be less her goal to preserve harmony between her parents, than to be apprehensive about her own loss of power. That is often the root of jealousy, particularly where there is no question of love, and where it is a matter of dividing relative power.

A few words may be said here about the extraordinary degree to which most neurotics cling to their families. Here we come upon a peculiarity which is found frequently in the general picture of a neurosis. The girl's form of expression is typical, *I idolized my parents and watched over them jealously.* Neurotics usually attach themselves closely to their family. That is certainly not to be adversely criticized. In general, it may be said that the final judgment of every human attitude and action may be based, on the one hand, on this attitude's content of social feeling or altruism, and on the other, on the content of the superiority striving or egoism. One and the same action can therefore be useful or useless, depending upon whether it works with, without or against social feeling. The degree of social feeling may be taken as a criterion for the level of human deeds and for the human being as well.

Now that we have seen that all neurotic characteristics are distinctly opposed to the social feeling, that the neurotic strives in a supremely egotistical manner for personal power at any price, we can well assume

SEXUAL DEVELOPMENT

that his devotion to his family is not based on sincere affection, but is used as a means to obtain an object to feed his lust for power. A nervous person needs the family which pities him, which believes in him, and thinks he is ill, as he needs his daily bread. He knows that he would be an absolute nonentity without his family, abandoned without hope of salvage to his feeling of insecurity and insufficiency. It is consequently to his advantage to make the ties between himself and his family as strong and lasting as possible, in which the usually uncritical attitude of his family helps him considerably. He often arranges an exaggerated affection for one or all the members of his family, which naturally has nothing at all to do with wishes tainted by incest. This arrangement gives him domination over the family, to the attainment of which end the family ties have been declared holy. In general, one finds nervous people more closely attached to their families than those who do not suffer from or complain of nervousness. The larger circle of the community frightens them back into the small circle of the family. Here he obtains what he does not believe himself capable of obtaining in a larger group. Wherever one meets a nervous person in the company of strangers, that is, outside the family, his gestures usually betray a backward tendency toward his family.

From this point, we may watch and see whether

THE CASE OF MISS R.

our general observations up to the present will be corroborated further in that part of the story which is yet to be read.

And he had to return home with me. And whenever he thought a girl pretty, I used to say, "All the women with monkey-faces seem to please you."

That is the expression of jealousy.

I came home one evening from the movies and found mother in great excitement. Father had gone to deliver some material. Mother told me that father's old assistant had been impudent and had wanted to attack her. I didn't quite understand what it was he wanted of her, but I was incensed and swore and cried, "That damn fellow—if I see him, I'll break his head!"

My best friend was my schoolmate Olga. She did everything I wanted her to do.

We might have guessed it.

We used to play theatre together.

There again is the emphasis on something visible. We have noticed before that this girl has an extraordinarily good visual sense, a penchant for everything visible. Those who have occupied themselves over a longer period of time with individual psychology, know that it can be proved that such an interest must

SEXUAL DEVELOPMENT

be trained. We have mentioned in a former paragraph that a training like this is usually started by some sight difficulty in early childhood or even in infancy. We may presume that something similar has been the matter with this child. Her visual training is unusually strong. Such points of special interest must be kept carefully in mind.

Many dramatists have had eye defects; their training has sprung from such defects. One must be able to see before one can visualize the presentation of a stage scene. This is easier for those who have placed seeing in the foreground. Such a training is a disadvantage when the difficulties are over-emphasized; on the other hand, an advantage can be seen in our appreciation of art.

We used to dress up in long robes, bind our heads with veils, and her brother was then a gypsy or a robber chief who stole me. Gradually he became annoying to me. He never wanted to let us alone.

You see here the stressed inclination to girls and the rejection of boys. He bothers her. One often finds an inclination like that. It shows a tendency toward members of the same sex. In addition, one must consider that girls develop more quickly than boys. If the boy was not much older, we can understand that the girls felt superior to him. That might also be a reason for rejecting him.

THE CASE OF MISS R.

Once I locked myself with her in her room. We undressed ourselves, jumped around naked, and examined ourselves all around in the mirror.

Again the desire to see.

And because we had heard somewhere or other that two together could do something impure, we laid ourselves, first one, then the other, on each other. We were very much disappointed because we didn't feel anything. Outside the door her brother cried.

Now we hear another reason. . . . At this point it is necessary to take up an important problem. Some one might speak of a homosexual component. Those psychological schools which believe in the inheritance of fully developed sexual tendencies, will conclude from the girl's last remembrance that the primordial urge which, fully developed, and dormant in her up to this moment, has finally broken through. Such a conclusion appears to us somewhat superficial and mechanistic. Our interpretation is different. We know that in childhood, as soon as sexual desire manifests itself, nothing is received with so much shock as the development of normal sex relations. The child's up-bringing and the impressions she receives from her environment have conspired at an early age to render shocking the first information about sexual relation between men and women. And what shocks a child will usually frighten it.

SEXUAL DEVELOPMENT

What is then more natural than that the sexual development of young people, which cannot be hindered, is hampered by nothing more than by normal relations and such sexual development is then diverted into abnormal channels? Such youngsters either begin to masturbate or they seek homosexual relations; but whatever form their sexuality may take, it is only the sordid remains of normal sexuality. Homosexuality and masturbation certainly are not the normal forms of sexual development. In such cases, the normal has been frightened out of existence by shock and anxiety. An example will prove our statement more definitely. Take those places where children are not watched too carefully, the poorhouses, for instance, where boys and girls are not separated. There you can find that no development of the sexual drive takes place other than the normal one. There you see children of five or eight years of age who have normal relations. Should one assume that well-to-do children develop sexually different from poor children? Or take those institutes which are exclusively for boys or girls and in which cases of homosexuality occur very often. Is it then just a coincidence that perverse sexual practices are more common among institutional children than among those who grow up in family homes, or is not the individual psychological conception more correct that the direction the sexual development of any individual takes is not

THE CASE OF MISS R.

inborn, but is determined by his environment and upbringing?

When a child masturbates, the parents are displeased and a spanking follows. But just imagine what would happen if a child really had normal relations. The bottom of the world would fall out. I remember that the development of those children who have dared has led inevitably to homosexuality because of the awful price they have had to pay. The children have been forced to refuse the normal, and the outcome of their sexual urge has been in the opposite direction.

And thus we can see the timid sexual expression of this girl in another light. The boy annoys her. Without knowing that, however, we may be assured that she will not increase her sexual experience by approaching boys; she is much too fearful for that. Thus she uses her friend Olga who, as she admits, did everything she wanted her to do and whom she likes for that very reason.

I don't remember who told me that love dies when one gives another a needle. Anyway, I believed it. I talked it over with Olga and we decided to use this magic on her brother. I took a needle, broke it in two, gave him one half and told him that that made our friendship stronger and that it meant being true to each other forever after. He took his half of the needle happily and stuck it in his jacket. Then I

SEXUAL DEVELOPMENT

laughed and said: "Now I can tell you that it's all over with love because the needle really means that love has been punctured!"

What did the boy do?

He began to cry bitterly.

He was obviously advanced in his development.

I was almost sorry for him. After a while it occurred to me to tell him that a gypsy had once prophesied that I would die when I was eighteen.

This theme of having an appointed time when she claims she must die, recurs frequently. We ask our key-question: what happens when she makes this claim? and we then begin to see through the veil: (1) if she really believes it, she feels herself superior to and excused from the prosaic duties of everyday existence. That is the end result. No matter what happens, there are no more tasks for her, a situation which suits a spoiled child; (2) when a girl makes such a statement, she immediately becomes the center of interest. Every one is so disturbed that the girl is treated with more indulgence than ever—the consequence of her desire for indulgence.

The boy was inconsolable. Tears rolled down his cheeks. I was also very much distressed. I had said it so convincingly that I almost believed it myself.

103

THE CASE OF MISS R.

I do not know whether I have as yet emphasized this peculiarity of the girl. Lying is quite common among neurotics. A pathological liar believes it when he says, "Our family is going to ruin." He feels it so much that he is shattered by it. A human being has the ability to make himself believe what he says. But just because all lies are not conscious lies (as, for example, in neurotic and psychotic cases) they should not be treated with severity and punishment, but, like all neurotic symptoms, with understanding and explanation. Neurotic lying is always an attempt to appear greater than one really is. It is therefore a sign of discouragement and an effort toward seeming greatness. The more a man believes he must lie, the more deeply he must be able to identify himself with the object of his lies in order to appear so credible—to himself and the other—that his story is absolutely convincing.

Speaking of identification, we cannot perceive or apperceive without identifying ourselves. Funny as it may sound, I have the feeling that I can identify myself with a hat. Or, for instance, playing ninepins and watching the ball rolling, one begins to sway as if one were the ball oneself. A feeling of this nature which one assumes or into which one talks oneself, as it were, is of much greater significance than has been heretofore supposed. Identification will, of course, come strongly to the fore when it shows it-

SEXUAL DEVELOPMENT

self suitable for the goal in view. The girl likes to see the boy cry and tells her story all the more convincingly.

The boy was crazily in love with me. I am still surprised that a child of nine years can love so much.

We see here a love experience in a child of eight years. Those who have their eyes open will not wonder. We recognize such tendencies in early youth. Many are honestly in love with the other sex at the age of four or six.

I made Minna's acquaintance in the park. Her father was a checker in a café. She invited me to her house. She had her own playroom, loads of toys, a child's dinner service, a little sideboard, even a set of doll's dishes, and always money for sweets.

We can imagine the consequences. She with her two poverty-stricken rooms, the other girl with the luxurious apartment—there will be difficulties. She will feel herself unable to invite the other. She will have to lie.

And now the following bothered me. Minna waited quite a while for an invitation from me. I was ashamed to have her at my house because we only had one room and a kitchen, lived so poorly and had no pretty furnishings. Once when we were standing in front of my house, I said to her, "Look

THE CASE OF MISS R.

up there, at the first story, there is our apartment. The whole floor belongs to us, but mother keeps the key. We also have a room on the parlor floor, but there isn't much room there." And she looked up curiously. I always had an excuse. One day I couldn't keep my appointment with her. I had to do an errand and couldn't let her know in time. She waited and waited in front of the house and I didn't appear. Finally she screwed up enough courage to enter the house and to knock on our door. I was very much embarrassed to see her in the house upon my return. But I saw at once that she felt quite at home and that reassured me. In the course of our conversation she asked me if we couldn't go upstairs. I replied quickly, "Not to-day, it hasn't been cleaned." Soon after, however, she learned the truth, and we both laughed at my pretensions. We met almost every day and I neglected Olga. We liked most to play at cooking. We used to mix chocolate and slices of apples with milk and eat the mess. We used to buy "charlotte russes" and pickles. And for a trifle we could go to the movies. When children were not allowed to enter, we would become furious and swear at the theatre owner. Then we used to read fairy tales together and also books which were not suitable for our age. I remember a book I found in a chest, "Julia's Marriage," by Prevost. It tells the story of a bridal night and I almost broke my head over it. And

106

SEXUAL DEVELOPMENT

once I got hold of a book, "Children of the Divorced,"
—the love and life story of a twelve or thirteen-year
old boy. He committed suicide at the end, and that
made me very sad. I couldn't understand the reason
for it. And I even read Ibsen in the fourth school
year, naturally without understanding him. For ex-
ample, I couldn't understand why Hedda Gabler shot
herself.

Adults frequently do not understand why either.

I wanted to learn from the books, to learn to un-
derstand human nature.

This reveals the secret of many of those children
who constantly read books. They want to fill the
gaps in their knowledge of their fellow human beings.
Children do not accept everything sight unseen; they
test and compare; they imitate what they see in the
moving pictures and in the theatre. They continually prepare for the rôle of the adult; they train in
every direction. One of these trainings lies in experiencing other people's fate from books. The strong-
est interest in beautiful literature arises from the fact
that we can see how another attempts to solve his
problems.

In the meantime, father had established himself as
an independent tailor. Our apartment served the
double purpose of workroom and living quarters,

THE CASE OF MISS R.

which cramped us very much. Otherwise things did not go so very badly with us. Father could even assume the responsibility of new furniture on the installment plan, two chests, a table, chairs and beds. Before Christmas there was so much to do that mother, who had continually to help father, found no time to cook. That annoyed me very much.

This child is anxious that everybody minds his business.

Minna's mother made the most elaborate preparations. They had been baking at her house for days; at our house sewing. On Christmas Eve mother went with father to deliver the finished suits. Lina, who had moved away because of the limited apartment space, took me with her to her house. There was a tiny Christmas tree. Everything was very nice, but the evening meal consisted only of herring, which didn't particularly attract me. When my parents called for me, I complained, "On Christmas Eve I have to eat herring." Father answered that he had enough money, and we were going to eat in a restaurant. But I had lost all desire. There was a Christmas tree at home and I also got what I wanted, a child's set of dishes like Minna's and a rattler, but the mood had been destroyed.

She is severe; when everything does not go smoothly, her mood is destroyed.

108

SEXUAL DEVELOPMENT

I visited Minna the following day. She had a large Christmas tree with electric candles, and innumerable presents lay on her table. I did not envy her on that account. . . .

This lack of envy might be pride.

. . . but when her mother asked me what I had received, I suddenly assumed the rôle of one to be pitied and said, "Nothing at all."

There lies the suppressed resentment, and at the same time the gesture of a beggar. We must watch this trait.

To belittle oneself in order to produce a greater effect is the beggar's attitude.

I was very much pitied and every one hurried to make me a present—a book of fairy tales and all sorts of pretty cakes. Among my father's customers was a young man who was friendly with a divorcée. This woman had a daughter of my age, who resembled me very much. Her mother took a great fancy to me and often used to take me out. She rented a villa for the summer in a suburb and invited me to visit her. Father let me go reluctantly. Minna was away in the country for the summer and this suburb was for me my first country vacation, and for a long time the only one. In spite of the fact that I was extremely well treated there, I became so homesick

109

THE CASE OF MISS R.

*after two days that I wept ceaselessly and demanded
to be allowed to return home.*

One must say something here about the psychology
of homesickness. No one is homesick who does not
feel that he is in a more favorable position at home.
Spoiled children are usually homesick. Her position
in the country seems to be a favorable one, but it is
really less so; at home she is the center, in the country only a little girl; therefore the homesickness. One
must yield to such homesickness; she was not prepared for the change in her situation.

*There was nothing else to do but to bring me home
again as soon as possible.*

*Lina studied for a whole year to be a nurse and
how to assist at operations, and smelled dreadfully
of carbolic acid. She fell in love with a Czech. Now
and then she would send me to him with a note. Once
the housekeeper opened the door and said, "You are
Miss Rosa's sister, aren't you?" and told me some gos-
sip.*

How soon this child of the people is initiated into
love relationships!

*I told my sister about Rosa, but she, of course, al-
ready knew about it. She often cried, and then father
and I would have to console her. When the Czech returned to his country, she took a position in a hos-*

SEXUAL DEVELOPMENT

pital in Prague to be near him. We tried in vain to dissuade her. Her departure irritated me exceedingly.

Why? She loses a person from her court. When we exaggerate the situation somewhat, we arrive at an anxiety neurosis which brings with it the necessity of such a person's having a court around her. She does not consciously realize that by this procedure she assumes an extremely powerful position.

CHAPTER VII

THE PROBLEM OF LOVE

I HAVE forgotten to mention Tilda, my first friend. I met her on the street.

In spite of the pampering she received it was possible for her to make the acquaintance of children on the street. There is probably no other way by which a child can learn so much of human nature and to distinguish people as on the street. If we could at the same time prevent the dissemination of so much evil knowledge it would be a good way to rear children. If it were possible to arrange for more supervision, if we could be reasonably sure that certain evil elements would not interpose themselves to lead children astray, it appears to me that this is probably a better way than any other to obtain a many-sided experience. The common rivalry, the struggle to discover and influence the relationship of human beings —that is the origin of social life. Large cities to-day cannot give children any sort of street life because of traffic dangers.

We have frequently had occasion to remark that this girl is an excellent observer and it is quite possible

112

THE PROBLEM OF LOVE

that she has developed this ability by associating with children on the street. Even if she has not escaped developing in a neurotic direction she still has developed to an unusual degree the power to combine her perceptions.

Such abilities are trained to be used later as means for the easier attainment of the fictive goal. Again and again we perceive how valuable strength and talents, abilities and possibilities are spoiled and made worthless by a neurotic goal. Were a neurotic to turn into useful channels the collective strength and intelligence which he employs in pursuit of a neurotic goal, the diverted energy would probably be enough to make a genius of him.

She had just hitched onto a delivery wagon; I climbed on after her; we began to speak to each other, played together, and promised to meet each other at the same place the following day. Her mother had a candy store in our neighborhood. I met her again in the fourth year at school and saw her often. She told me of her suitor, a ten-year old boy, Henry by name, who had already promised to marry her.

We see how far-reaching the preparation for future life is, even in a child's tenth year.

When I made his acquaintance I immediately tried . . .

113

THE CASE OF MISS R.

To do what?

. . . to take him away from her.

This girl, who was accustomed to being first, had to choose this course when she found herself in such a situation.

I was half successful. We three went to the movies together, used to steal into the garden of the insane asylum together and play at being married.

That is the beginning of sexual relations. These plays, doctor play, mother and father play, parents and children play, can be found among children the world over. The children make them up themselves. I wonder that no one has as yet discovered a repetition of forgotten, archaic rites in these games. It is superfluous to speculate upon the theory that each individual must repeat in himself the entire story of mankind, as some psychologists believe. Every individual is forced to use the same sort of games as a preparation and training for adulthood, and he does not have to repeat the whole story of mankind in order to do this.

We often spoke of a friend of Henry's who was very good-looking, but who was also quite arrogant and who didn't think much of girls.

We see how the variations in adult personalities are formed in early childhood. Children recognize

THE PROBLEM OF LOVE

these variations and also know how to react to them. Henry's friend made an impression on our heroine.

That sounded interesting to me and I asked Tilda to arrange to have us meet. When she spoke to him about it, he said he would look me over.

I do not know if all of my readers can comprehend how the girl is made to play a subordinate part. It does not need a long explanation to point out that the boy looked down on girls. His form of expression is degrading and it is so understood by the girl. He to whom this undertone is not audible, who is not musical enough to apprehend it, will not be able to grasp our way of thinking.

We all met. We walked around a bit and our talk was soon of kisses. I asserted that I would never in my life let myself be kissed by any one. The boy answered that he would prove the contrary to me, by force if necessary. I did not take him in earnest. It was already twilight when we crossed the square, and he threw his arms around me. I struggled, called to Tilda for help and freed myself after some effort.

The picture recurs. Man is the aggressor, the girl the hunted animal—how hard things are, how careful one must be to avoid such attacks.

I upbraided him for his impudence and pointed out that a stolen kiss was not the same as one given voluntarily.

115

THE CASE OF MISS R.

Notice how the ten-year old girl can argue; she has learned it in her family.

And that, if I were a boy, I would never bother about stealing a kiss.

With that she degrades him.

I walked alongside him cautiously. What angered me most was that he had rumpled my hat and hair. Soon after he asked for another appointment through Tilda, but I didn't care about seeing him again since I knew I could have him.

For the first time this girl is brought face to face with the problem of love. She must assume some sort of position in response. Unquestioningly, the form of response or reaction will be influenced to some extent by the behavior of the other person. Nevertheless, I believe we may definitely conclude from all that has gone before, and from the little test which we have just read, that our girl will not regard love as a means of development, and certainly not as an expression of social feeling, but as a means to win power and significance. On condition, naturally, that she does not run away from the problem completely. We have to watch carefully in her story how she reacts further to the question of love as one of the three great life problems—whether she approaches or withdraws from it. We can measure the degree

116

THE PROBLEM OF LOVE

to which a human being is normal or neurotic by the degree to which he attempts to solve or evades his problems.

During my fifth year at school, I became friendly with a girl named Sophie. She could play the piano and I was envious of her on that account.

We see how her striving for recognition proceeds in all directions.

I had long wanted a piano.

I know that here I shall hear the objection; is it a sin to want to play the piano? We find it quite worth while, but is that all? No matter what comes along, she will say, "I want to have that, too; I want to have that, too." This constant wanting is characteristic. There is nothing in the world which, when forced into the foreground to the exclusion or detriment of other factors, does not disturb the smooth course of one's existence. Cleanliness is worth while, but when I make it the salient feature in my life and think only of how to make everything clean, I then not only neglect all other important tasks, but I discover that everything is so dirty that it is not even worth the trouble to continue living. Thus constant washing becomes the symptom of a compulsion neurosis.* A

---

* A compulsion neurosis produces symptoms which the patient believes forces him to do certain things against his conscious will.

THE CASE OF MISS R.

person may say that everything is dirty. Is he right? We shall not discuss it. If we make that the most important thing in life we can no longer live.

It is the same with sexuality. When I make sexuality the pivot of my existence, the world is then so topsy-turvy that I don't know the difference between left and right. One person makes this problem of major importance, another individual chooses another problem to overemphasize. To understand this we must also understand that everything starts in early childhood and therefore must be false because children cannot approach the absolute truth and cannot judge the world correctly. Stressing one problem to the exclusion of others disturbs the harmony of life.

And still there is a principle which convinces me that overemphasis does not have to disturb life, and that is the principle of social feeling. When I keep to the standpoint that, under any circumstances, I will go only the way of general usefulness, I can make no important mistakes. No one has as yet been able really to disprove this principle.

There we hear the objection: the personality is lost. I must fashion myself in a form adjustable to my general environment. In the case at hand, however, we find a very much exaggerated striving for recognition. The goal of superiority is also expressed in the desire for a piano.

THE PROBLEM OF LOVE

Sophie's foster parents—her parents were dead—had a grocery store where mother often used to make her purchases. In this way the two families became acquainted with each other. Her mother suggested to my father that he send me to the same music school her daughter attended which boasted an excellent teacher. I could then practice at their house. Father took her suggestion and I entered the music school.

We should also like to remark here that this intense struggle to attain greater heights is neither to be hindered nor censured. We would all agree that she should learn to play and that everything was still in the direction of the generally useful.

Girls and boys were together at the school. Many of the boys fell in love with me. I thought they were all fools and ran away from them. One in particular never left me in peace. He always greeted me with "I kiss your hand, Fräulein." That pleased me somewhat, but otherwise I didn't like him because his father was a shoemaker.

Her father was a tailor. We see how significant social rank is to her. If her father had been a shoemaker, and his a tailor, she would have argued in the same way; that is to say, the shoemaker would then have been better. From this one sentence we can deduce that this girl wants to surpass every one, not only

THE CASE OF MISS R.

in the family, but in the outside community as well. As a consequence, she can give but little to the community. Her problem is; how can I be first? She stumbles upon obstacles and opposition. She must be careful not to fall in love for *hat and hair may be rumpled.*

I liked to make believe . . . that I was of better family and if I could avoid it, I never said that my father was a tailor. When I was younger and some one asked me what his occupation was, I used to answer that he was a fire engine inspector. Our boarder, who had been a fireman, often told us of fires and how dangerous a fireman's job was. That made a deep impression on me.

If he had told some heroic story, she would also have made use of it.

I treated the shoemaker's son badly. When I was in good humor, I permitted him to accompany me part way, but when I was in bad humor, he was not allowed to come near me. I used to say "sir" to him and order him about, "Just see that you go your own way, sir, or I'll call a policeman." That made him angry and he got two other boys to watch for me and throw stones at me. Then I would run away. I saw them waiting for me in the schoolhouse and that frightened me very much. I was afraid our

120

THE PROBLEM OF LOVE

teacher might see them and think that I had something to do with them.

Here appears the dread of a bad reputation. The expression of a trait which likewise appears in intensified form in a neurosis is, "What will the others say?" It is the anxious, consequent slogan of those who would be first. Almost all people live in fear of the opinion of others and permit their actions to be influenced by it. When we become aware of the unnecessarily great extent to which superfluous anxiety and worry govern the conduct of our fellow human beings, and of how little true courage there is in the world, we cannot wonder that our epoch is called the "neurotic age." It was probably not much different in other times; perhaps the only distinction is to be found in the changing fashions of living.

There was a high school student at the music school who used to lend me detective stories. Henry also used to lend me some. I devoured them with Olga or Sophie. Detective stories gradually became my passion. At night I was so terror-stricken that I couldn't sleep.

Many children prefer detective stories because they like the tense excitement produced by reading them and, further, because they like to discover tricks in

THE CASE OF MISS R.

such stories which they can utilize to achieve a certain sort of superiority over others.

It depends upon the type of book or the style of life of the reader as to what reasons are given for the fascination of detective stories. In most cases it appears that the reader likes to identify himself with the detective whose superior ability to uncover trails and detect clues, whose strength and dominating position are all so impressive. Here is a man who obviously knows nothing of impeding weakness in mind or body which makes so much trouble for the reader in his daily life. The reader, in his imagination, elevates himself to the rôle of a fictive personality (the detective) and obtains the laurels of success without exertion. The value of such identification lies often in the carrying over and retention in daily life of some of the courage inherent in the imagined rôle of the detective.

The fascination of detective stories lies as well in the excitement and anxiety evoked. The reader frequently finds himself in a tense state by having identified himself with the pursued, and this tension enables him to come upon ideas for saving himself. This is true especially of those books in which the author gives the rôle of hero or adventurer to the fugitive who must overcome innumerable obstacles in his path. The reader almost always identifies himself with the character to whom has been assigned the rôle of

THE PROBLEM OF LOVE

hero, no matter whether detective, adventurer or thief. Only those individuals who always do choose the opposite select a disagreeable character with which to identify themselves.

All readers extract some form of pseudo-superiority from detective, mystery or adventure stories. They like to play with dangers which are really no dangers for them and which, as they know in advance, they are going to conquer. They abstract, as it were, from reality without having to assume any responsibility. And therein lies the danger of fantastic tales. They estrange from reality and open the way to irresponsible, neurotic dreaming. Courageous individuals do not need such fictions and will not resort to them.

I was also passionately fond of films dealing with criminals. One of the theatres once gave "The Man in the Cellar." Children were denied admission. I schemed the whole day how to get in. Finally I got one of the older girls to buy a ticket for me, pulled my hat down over my face and got in.

You see the effect of the detective stories and crime films.

The picture had a terrible effect on me. I couldn't fall asleep for a whole week. I was afraid to breathe in the dark. I would wake mother up, and when she fell asleep, I would then awaken father.

THE CASE OF MISS R.

This tendency to disturb her parents in the night has been known to us for some time. When her mood became one of anxiety through identifying herself with the characters in the moving picture, the result was that which her style of life compelled. The result would have been the same without the feeling of anxiety, but with it, she only feels herself the more justified.

Terrible fear also caused the following:

We observe how this girl begins to describe how she gathers anxieties as a miser gathers treasure and how she collects situations which can produce anxiety.

Father had the habit of letting the shutters down but not closing them. Every passerby could look in. Once I was lying awake in bed between my parents. Father was still reading. He used to read an hour before going to sleep. And suddenly I saw two eyes which glared into the room like those of one crazed.

The erotic reason for the peeping can be recognized distinctly from the manner in which the girl describes the incident. When she speaks of horrible shocks, we must not forget her tendency to harp upon and exaggerate situations producing anxiety.

I was very ambitious and learned quickly during my first three years at school. I liked best chorus

124

THE PROBLEM OF LOVE

practice. I didn't have a good voice, but had a good ear. Some children always sang off key.

Here also we see how sharply she notes the difference between herself and others. This difference would not had had such significance for another that it would have been remembered.

They trembled when called upon to sing and didn't even dare open their mouths.

She has recognized very well the unfortunate inferiority feeling of those children who lack some accomplishment, and who lose control of themselves when they must reveal this lack. I have seen children almost desperate because they could not whistle. I once met a boy who told me that he could not whistle for a long time. One day he succeeded in whistling and felt as if God were going to whistle through him. We can see from this description what immense importance is ascribed to these abilities.

They made me laugh so much that I had to stick my head under my seat.

We have known for some time that laughter is also a language and has significance. Dostoievski says that one can tell a man's character from the way he laughs. She laughs so heartily that she must hide her head under the chair. That looks as if it would pain her to show the others how superior she is. He who

THE CASE OF MISS R.

can recall the picture of a classroom knows that nothing is more noticeable than hiding one's head beneath one's bench. It is an exaggeration which looks more harmless than it really is.

And sometimes I laughed so much that a little accident would happen. . . . When I was ten years old, in the fourth year at school, I began to neglect my schoolwork. I became lazy, inattentive and very dreamy.

We do not know why this girl grew less studious in her fourth school year. She may have had another teacher whom she liked less; maybe she was scolded. Suddenly she applied the brakes and stopped. It often happens that spoiled children progress as long as the way is smooth, and neglect their work as soon as a difficulty presents itself.

The teacher said I could have been one of the best students but that I was too lazy.

She is fully satisfied with that. That is the pronouncement which often attracts children to laziness; they satisfy themselves with the possibility. They do not speculate badly. "One bird in the hand is worth two in the bush," is taken to be the greatest wisdom. The feeling, "I could be the best," is sufficient; they do not go further so as not to destroy this illusion. When they really accomplish something they have the advantage of being praised by the

THE PROBLEM OF LOVE

others; those children who are consistently studious are not noticed so much. Lazy children stumble upon a paying road; like all unmanageable children, they work under less trying conditions.

Father was indifferent to my progress at school. He only concerned himself with my health. He was always careful to see that I had enough fresh air. In the evening, when he was through working, he often went walking with me. We would pace quickly along the streets to the railroad viaduct. Then I waited, shuddering, until the train shot out of the tunnel. It could be heard thundering a long way off. It appeared to me like a monster, a dragon, a devil. The moment it rushed passed me, I swore at it out of the smoke which threatened to obscure me.

Even this little incident is exaggerated, comparisons made to increase the effect of the sight of the train. Even out of that she extracts the advantage of the possibility for anxiety. She will construct bugbears until she will not be able to rid herself of her anxiety. That is the development and training towards an anxiety neurosis.

I was not a good student in high school either. When Christmas came during my first year at high school, I wanted a piano badly. Father wanted to buy me a second-hand one, but could not find any good enough. Christmas morning had already come.

127

THE CASE OF MISS R.

I cried, yelled, scolded, threatened neither to eat nor drink if there were no piano in the house by evening.

It is not to be doubted that her relation even to her father is poisoned by her desire to rule.

At that time father's earnings were quite good and he had intended to buy me a piano anyway. When I became so wildly furious, he dressed himself and promised that he would try to buy one on the installment plan. After some delay he succeeded in getting one and it arrived just in time. I was never so happy in my life. I immediately opened it and began to play. Then I ran over to Sophie and invited her to return with me and see it. And then I played again and played and played until father made me stop. I was really happy that day. The next day I arose very early and practiced diligently. Before that I had always said that I had a piano. Now I didn't have to lie any more.

I used to play pieces for four hands with Sophie. At the end of the year a concert was arranged at the music school. I wanted to be nicely dressed for it and asked for white shoes. Father didn't want to buy me any and painted an old pair white for me. The general examination took place at the school on a Sunday morning. We played our pieces. We even had to learn to bow correctly. Everything went off smoothly. I had no stage fright and played my pieces

THE PROBLEM OF LOVE

*without any mistakes. I played one piece with So-
phie.*

We should like to use the opportunity to say a few
words about stage fright. Stage fright is a very frequent symptom. In general it may be said that stage
fright usually appears when people who are confronted with a task, are less concerned with the accomplishment of the task than with worry about
what people are going to say about them. We have
already seen that many neurotics are greatly dependent upon the opinions of others. When their striving
to accomplish something extraordinary is excessively
intensified, the success of this striving becomes in-
creasingly uncertain and the possibility of failure
looms that much nearer. What is clearly apparent in
stage fright is the general, neurotic anxiety before a
decision, the hesitating attitude, and the distance between the person frightened and his fellow human
beings. If that pinnacle of success which inordinate
ambition has set is not achieved, stage fright offers
an excellent alibi. If the task (a speech, an examination, or whatever it may be) is crowned with success, the value of such a success is doubled, for it has
been attained in spite of the handicap of stage fright.

There are various reasons for the absence of stage
fright, before a public appearance. Either such absence is a sign of a perfect objectiveness and adjustment to life, or it is routine training, or it is the

THE CASE OF MISS R.

naïveté of one who has never suffered a defeat. Stage fright is naturally no inborn characteristic, but results from early experiences. The reason for the absence of stage fright in this girl is unquestionably the last named, that is, the naïveté of one who has never suffered a defeat. We can imagine how it will be when she is confronted with a failure or with a dangerous situation. As long as she continues to progress, she has no stage fright.

My friend distinguished herself and recited a poem at the end of the performance. A year later we found, in addition, that something practical and lucrative could be done with my piano playing. Tilda's father, Mr. Stockinger, who was a waiter in a wine restaurant, suggested that we play together in the restaurant. One evening Tilda and I collected our music, small pieces, quadrilles, waltzes, and so on and went over to the restaurant. We lost our courage at the entrance. We quarrelled as to who should enter first and squeezed through together. Mr. Stockinger immediately brought us to a table and gave us some wine. Then we were asked to go to the piano. At first we were too shy. After some coaxing, however, we went to the piano, and looking neither left nor right, began to pound the keys. There was much applause and that flattered us. After a short pause, we played the second piece in our best style. When we had gone through our repertoire, we took a plate and

THE PROBLEM OF LOVE

went around collecting money which we later divided. We bought a lot of chocolate and cake on the way home. I gave father a silver coin.

There was a restaurant next door to us in which an athletic society met every Wednesday and Saturday. They always engaged a musician to play for them. I often saw the men exercising. They made the funniest faces when they marched to the music and when they exercised with the heavy iron dumb-bells which they couldn't quite manage to raise aloft completely. Their arms trembled and their bellies shook. I could hardly restrain my laughter.

How she tried to revenge herself on those who were strong. She would like to laugh them all out of countenance and always finds a reason for laughing at them.

The musician was ill once and the restaurant owner didn't know what to do about getting a substitute on such short notice. He thought of me. I was quite willing since I could earn a little money.

Something should be said here about the desire of children to earn money. Children have an intense longing to earn money and one must try to turn this longing in the proper direction. We can discover the same longing in adults who have always been financially dependent upon others and who have never earned any money themselves. It is wrong to

THE CASE OF MISS R.

speak here of miserliness, thrift, or the desire for money per se. We see it better in the light of individual psychology. It is the struggle for equality. Since money has, in our civilization, become the measure of a man's worth, even though a most inadequate one, everybody exerts himself to realize his worth in money. In this way we understand the child's desire for money and the possession of money as the endeavor to be equal.

The athletes were pleased with me and offered me tarts and beer. One of the men was very fat. Later I received another tip. At home I assumed all sorts of airs, snubbed my family, answered their questions nervously, and then told them they ought to have some consideration for me after the strain of such hard work.

We see how this girl begins to assume airs. She has done it before in order to appear greater.

I substituted for the pianist as long as he was ill, and later played once in a while when he was away. There was hardly room to move in our tiny flat. An apartment was vacant in Sophie's house which had an additional room, and the living room and kitchen were also larger there. We moved over, but my proximity to Sophie lasted only a short time. For some reason or other, the landlord gave Sophie's parents notice. Her parents sold their store and moved to Ot-

THE PROBLEM OF LOVE

*takring, quite some distance away from us. I visited
her often. She told me about a boy with whom she
had fallen in love and pointed him out to me. I sur-
veyed him and then gave her my opinion. "I wouldn't
have anything to do with a boy like that. Get him
out of your head."*

We are already familiar with this attitude. What
another has is worthless.

*That didn't stop me from flirting with him. . . .
I always dressed myself carefully when I went over
to see her and would parade in front of her. She admired me very much.*

There we have the ideal friend for this girl. Her
friend must admire her, must put up with criticism
and let herself be ordered about.

*She adored me. She took literally whatever I said.
She met a girl in her new neighborhood whom we
both mocked. Sophie explained to me that she only
went around with her because she was bored, but that
she always thought of me. To make her jealous, I
told her that I had fallen in love with a boy, described
him in detail, and told her how we kissed and how
we talked to each other in the movies. I said he was
surely going to marry me. And I promised her that
I would hide her under my bed on my bridal night
and she promised to do the same in case she married
before I did.*

THE CASE OF MISS R.

Again her penetrating curiosity.

Then we kissed each other and swore always to be true to one another. She often complained of her foster father. He used to tell nasty jokes which thoroughly disgusted her. He even wanted to "touch" her. She was very much afraid of him. I shuddered when I heard this. Her foster father was also very strict; he boxed her ears when she brought a bad report card from school. My father would laugh and say, "Five is more than one." (Five was a bad mark, one a good mark.) *I once got a mark of five in the class on religion. It happened this way. I had not gone to mass on Sunday and had to give a suitable excuse. Instead of doing that, when I was asked why I had not attended, I replied, "Because I didn't want to."*

We know that in school nothing is more dangerous than to tell the truth about such things. As long as one lies, one is respectable, but when one tells the truth, then one is a culprit. I do not know how children emerge from this training in school. Woe to the child who says, "I was bored," or who answers the question, "Why didn't you greet me?" with "Because I didn't want to." When he lies, he is a valued member of human society; when he tells the truth, he is lost.

Here we see a further reason why children lie. Often it is the way of least resistance. Children learn

THE PROBLEM OF LOVE

to save themselves many disagreeable moments by lying. They sometimes have the example of an adult whom they detect in a lie and whom they then imitate. In the latter event, there is the added attraction of being able to imitate an adult, or, in other words, to appear greater than one really is.

The class was as still as a mouse. It sounded like blasphemy. It was at least honest. Only the teacher didn't know enough to appreciate my honesty.

We understand how this girl came to do it. She must also feel superior to her teacher.

I believe that was in the first class at public school. At that time father had a book with pictures illustrating the whole story of the persecution of the Christians in Rome. I couldn't read very well at that time so he explained the pictures and told me the whole story. I would arrange stage scenes with my doll. Most of the time she would take the part of a king's daughter. Presumably under the influence of those pictures which presented the crucifixion, I composed the following play: a strange knight steals my doll and kisses her in front of her husband who has just come in. Her husband starts to scream. The knight, with the consent of the stolen princess (the doll) has the husband knifed by a couple of hangman's assistants, tortured with heated tongs, and then orders his skin torn off. And while I was imag-

135

THE CASE OF MISS R.

ining all that to myself, I suddenly had the most peculiar feeling.

There we have the emerging of a sadistic-sexual fantasy. She is only an onlooker, but there is the inclination in her always to observe how badly it fares with some one else. We have often remarked how she attempts to degrade others. There are two things to be considered in attempting to explain how she comes to create such images: (1) her father, with the story of the persecution of Christians, has really opened the door for sexual stimulation under cover of sadistic, painful scenes and pictures; (2) she discovers at the same time that she belongs to that type which, at the sight of such scenes is not affected by accelerated heartbeat, gooseflesh, or loss of control of the sphincter muscles (muscles controlling discharge of bodily waste), but is stimulated sexually. We gather that her anxiety dreams, her liking for criminal films, do not remain merely as anxiety images in her, but go further and excite her erotically.

When the feeling subsided, I got up and thought to myself, "Now you have made a marvellous discovery. No one suspects what a wonderful feeling such images can produce."

We have heard how she was in the process of training herself in the production of anxiety images and

THE PROBLEM OF LOVE

now that her type takes clearer form, she begins to train more strongly in this direction.

The first time I really heard anything about sexual intercourse was in the first high school class. There was a clique of girls in that class who had matured at an early age and had well-developed bodies. They were supposed to understand jokes with a double meaning and to go around with boys. During rest periods they could always be seen whispering to each other. I wanted to learn what they knew, so I approached them, behaved like them in order to win their confidence and walked home from school with them.

It happens frequently that children pretend to know more than they really do in order to learn something. Here we see quite clearly how information concerning sex spreads in school. I am convinced that there is no means by which we can prevent it. Whatever he who attempts to explain sex to children does in an effort to combat such dissemination is useless against the elementary force which pervades the school. At that age children are critical and do not believe everything.

When I was finally alone with one girl who was supposed to know very much, I asked her if she knew where children came from. She said yes. I begged her

THE CASE OF MISS R.

to tell me. I had heard different things but didn't believe them. She didn't want to tell me at first. I teased her so long, however, that she finally consented. I had to swear that I would never tell any one.

Notice how the girl who is supposed to be the most experienced is ashamed and embarrassed and how she demands that it be kept a secret.

Then she put her head close to mine, walked up and down with me, and said that one must have sexual intercourse in order to have a child. The expression "sexual intercourse" was not clear to me, so she described the procedure. Horrified, I cried, "That can't be true!"

CHAPTER VIII

THE SHOCK OF SEX KNOWLEDGE

INDIVIDUAL PSYCHOLOGY has always believed that man is an indivisible whole, a more or less concentrated bundle of life, striving toward a goal. To attain this goal he constructs a system into which he takes everything that may help him further and by which he rejects all that may hinder his progress. When a man has an experience and this experience registers in his memory, it becomes a part of and belongs to his system. This system always exists, and there is no form of expression which does not belong to it. The life of an ordinarily healthy person conceals this system, serious mental disorders reveal it distinctly. Psychiatrists have long recognized the rigid schematicism of mental illnesses, especially noticeable in paranoia. Individual psychological investigations have gone a step further and have pointed out that a similar life scheme is present in every human being, with the modification that in relatively normal individuals it is not so prominently noticeable.

When we apply this idea to our story, we come

139

THE CASE OF MISS R.

much nearer to a realization of this girl's system. Up to the present we have been able to harmonize every trait and every expression with her system. We are dealing here with a spoiled child who always wants to occupy the leading position and who wants to avoid every situation which does not fit into her style of life. Let us see whether our postulate is justified.

My lack of confidence seemed to offend her somewhat, so she described the whole thing to me again. Then I wanted to know if only certain people had intercourse, or really everybody.

This is one of the customary questions asked by children as soon as they learn something of sex.

She answered, "Everybody, otherwise there would be no children," and then promised to tell me more about it the next time.

Here we now have the point of which I have often spoken. . . . One should not believe that explanations by children are more pernicious than those by learned adults. When you compare the explanations given by children and by scientists, you will often prefer the children's explanation. Their description is more human, more delicate. This child does not have to believe the other who is supposed to know more; she can doubt and in this way prepare herself for the truth. When an adult with his officious au-

140

THE SHOCK OF SEX KNOWLEDGE

thority, comes and gives a brusque and dogmatic explanation, the child has no time for preparation, no time to doubt, to adjust, or to protect itself. You have only to examine a pamphlet on sexual enlightenment to see that children are more delicate.

In spite of the exact description, I still doubted her words. It seemed too piggish to me. I came home quite excited. The more I thought about it, the more the alleged intercourse seemed grotesque. I grew nauseous when I thought of all other people, I excepted my parents, for I really didn't believe they would do anything so filthy. It even occurred to me that it was probably a dirty joke which some man had concocted and spread about.

You see the attempt to soften the blow.

I did think, however, that it was quite beyond good people, and in particular, my parents, to do anything of the sort. And a girl who would permit herself to do that was, in my eyes, contaminated and degraded. It was inconceivable to me how one could live after it.

Here appears the snag which it does not seem possible to avoid in enlightening a child on sex, since the child already has a fixed form of life. When such a child strives to be foremost, to shine in every respect, it receives the impression from such an explanation that sex is concerned with something debasing and it

THE CASE OF MISS R.

will, sooner or later, protect itself from the approach of the opposite sex. Even the most careful explanation cannot avoid this danger. The degree to which she will repel advances will depend upon how much she has fed her ambition. She will have difficulties, will begin to resent her sex. The superiority of the feminine rôle appears to be threatened and this is due to our culture which grants men privileges whereby they appear superior in sexual intercourse. It is a lie in our culture. If we could stamp it out, permit men no privileges and achieve equality there would then be no place for the thought of debasement or inferiority. But "to wash and not get wet" is impossible. If I were to believe that this pitfall could be avoided by explanation, I should be manifesting a superlative naïveté.

It was incomprehensible that people could go on living afterwards.

We can imagine that a girl, so fiercely ambitious, will try her utmost to ward off all thoughts of love and marriage. She will struggle desperately to avoid any solution, when these thoughts become a serious problem. She will appear like some one who has set herself the task of building up a life from which love and marriage are excluded.

How I myself came to be I did not think of at all.

That is one of the forms in which the rejection of

THE SHOCK OF SEX KNOWLEDGE

the feminine rôle, the elimination of sexual activity, makes itself manifest. She did not think. What she does is active and difficult work. It is mental strain. Neither to see nor to think nor to be face to face with the question: How did I come to be?

I confided to Sophie what I had learned and added that I couldn't believe it. Then she told me that some time ago she had heard her parents' bed creaking loudly. She couldn't see anything because it was too dark, but the creaking was very suspicious—her parents surely had an intercourse. I made her describe the creaking in detail. Then I said to her "It may be well with your parents, but mine surely don't do it. I lie between them in bed and I should have noticed something long before this. My father is entirely too proper anyway. He originally wanted to be a priest.

You see how her first reaction is a thought which comes primarily from her longing for superiority. Just as she didn't say before that her father was a tailor, now she surrounds him with the glory of having wanted to be a priest.

Soon after I again walked home with my knowing schoolmate. She told me a whole lot more, all of which was disgusting to me; that all married women had intercourse; that it hurt very much the first time and that one bled the first time; that prostitutes did it for money and then had operations in order not to

143

THE CASE OF MISS R.

have any children; and that men wore a rubber protector.

You see we are now in the realm of sexual clarification.

Another girl said later that she had a thick medical book at home which she used to read secretly. Sexual intercourse was explained in that book in detail as well as the sexual organs, and there were pictures in addition. I asked her to lend me the book. She answered that she was afraid her parents might discover that the book was missing or that my parents might discover the book in my possession. I persuaded her that everything would be kept secret and she promised to let me have the book for two hours.

A frequent procedure during the time of sexual clarification is to look in books. The dictionary plays an important rôle.

She invited me to her house. We wrapped the book in newspapers and I carried it with a beating heart to my house and hid it beneath a chest. After supper I got it out and sat down in a corner. My parents were very busy just then and didn't watch me. I read with boundless excitement. Now I had it in black on white and could do nothing but accept the sexual act as a fact. But I still thought my parents incapable of doing any such thing. And I decided then never to marry.

THE SHOCK OF SEX KNOWLEDGE

You see we have here the confirmation of what we expected, so that we can anticipate precisely what she is going to do or not to do, according to the style of life developed up to now. She collects reasons to avoid love in which she fears a defeat.

On the rare occasions when father and mother were affectionate to each other, I would throw myself energetically between them and give them to understand that I alone was the one to receive caresses.

Here also is a vigorous reaction against sexuality. When one assumes that she does this because she is jealous of her mother and wants her mother's place in relation to her father, one disturbs the clear unity of her behavior pattern. Childish jealousy of one of the parents, when a member of the opposite sex, was called by Freud the Œdipus complex. Œdipus was a Greek who unknowingly married his mother after he had killed his father. We believe that only in a few cases is childish jealousy based on sexual reasons. In general, the jealousy of children does not express desire for sexual possession of father or mother, but merely a wish to occupy a higher and more powerful position. It is an expression of the struggle for superiority.

During the night I lay like a Cerberus between them. I often remained awake for hours—not purposely to watch. I simply fell asleep with difficulty.

THE CASE OF MISS R.

And when father snored, I tickled him with my braid and when mother snored, I shook her. I couldn't stand snoring.

A partial diversion from the theme. Even here there is nothing but I and again I. Everything must happen as *I* want it. One can often find in the later lives of adults that they cannot bear certain habits, for example, snoring. Our girl objects to disturbances like snoring or turning on the light. One sees how the lust for power is mirrored in these trivialities. The slightest occasion is seized as an opportunity to lay down a law for another. One can see most distinctly the powerful compulsion in the demand for quiet. That is one of the means most resorted to. It is a means which appears modest, but which is, in reality, tyrannical. As if such a thing as quiet were possible. The other must pattern his life rules on mine; he must live so that my demands become his general maxime.

When it grew dark the prostitutes used to walk the streets. I watched them now with entirely different eyes. I wished I could hide myself in the room of one of them to see what happened. And once when it was evening, there was a man standing outside a house on the street and his trousers were open.

Such persons are called exhibitionists. They are cowards in life who avoid normal sexual relationship and arrive at their sordid satisfaction by exhibiting

146

THE SHOCK OF SEX KNOWLEDGE

their sexual organs to desirable women, usually young girls. They are excited by the fright and the nervousness aroused in the girl; they extract a cheap triumph from their seeming power to force another human being into a wretched situation.

There are probably few girls and women who have never encountered an exhibitionist. It is a frequent occurrence of which men are less aware. I have learned from personal experience that it is a widespread abuse. It makes a strong impression on such a girl and she is diverted still further from the normal road.

In telling her story she knows that she is stepping on the road of desertion. While she plans and follows her behavior pattern, she lays one brick after another, cemented by her striving for superiority and her fight to exclude everything which does not fit into her system.

I screamed and ran away madly. I never ran so quickly in my life.

You see with what force it is emphasized. It is the flight which will be manifest in everything and everywhere.

When I was in the second year at high school, I suddenly imagined that the calves of my legs were too thin. . . .

147

THE CASE OF MISS R.

That is doubt of one's own beauty. This girl doubts easily. If she were to imagine that she was pretty, it would be an impulse in the direction of love. If she were to make her longed-for superiority a reality, she might be forced to face and accept a problem.

It might be objected here that she is taking pains to make herself prettier, that she really wants to attract men, eventually to have a normal relationship. It is true that she wants to attract, but only to secure her superiority. At the very bottom she doubts whether she is really attractive enough to make some one love her. And this doubt is more important than all the useless puttering about which seems to flatter her vanity. This doubt is arranged. We must not forget that doubt does not come from heaven, it fits exactly into a person's system. There are two ways of looking at doubt. Either we doubt because there is some unsolved problem, or we doubt in order to have an excuse for evading a decision.

Our girl needs doubt in her system and therefore she makes such discoveries of which we shall doubtless hear more.

. . . and put on three pairs of stockings. Father was angry about it because it was summer and he said my feet would perspire. So I cut off the feet of the stockings and only wore the top parts. Then I stuffed them with cotton and even put on a pair of father's knitted trunks.

THE SHOCK OF SEX KNOWLEDGE

Apart from the fact that this procedure springs from a doubt of one's power to attract, it is a symptom of a nervous condition already known to us. It is an activity on the useless side of life. It is an over-emphasis of useless things. The harmony of life destroyed by it.

My arms too

You see how that progresses.

. . . seemed to me too thin.

We are prepared for the fact that she will find many ugly points about herself with consequence "I cannot marry; I must exclude love completely from my life." She gathers reasons like a bee honey in order to shirk.

I wouldn't have gone out with a short-sleeved dress for anything. Then I imagined I had snaky hands. So I tried to hide my hands as much as possible. At school there were girls with curved bodies. There was nothing to see on me. Olga and I measured our chests with tapemeasures. The result was very discouraging. Then we stuffed our bosoms with handkerchiefs and paraded on the street.

That looks like an attempt to attract others. In connection with other facts, however, we perceive that this girl considers herself of little worth. She

THE CASE OF MISS R.

makes attempts, as she says, to improve her appearances. In these attempts is hidden a deep feeling of inferiority. No matter what she has done up to now there is nowhere an indication in the direction of love and marriage. Such attempts are sufficient for parading on the street, but not sufficient for marriage.

Once when I passed my hand over my head, it seemed to me pointed and angular.

Now she is at the end of her art. She can stuff her stockings to make her calves appear larger, she can stuff her dress front to swell her bosom, but what of the head? You see how this training goes on. Up to her head everything had been patchwork; she must come to the point where she proves to herself that she is not suited for love.

I used to keep my hat on as long as I could. Sometimes the perspiration would run down underneath and I would not take it off. I remember now that when I was eight years old, I forgot to take off my hat in the class room. The teacher had to remind me of it.

At this point it would be advantageous to say something more about remembered and forgotten facts. We have already seen the certain conclusions can be drawn from remembrances, and incidents in

150

THE SHOCK OF SEX KNOWLEDGE

an individual's style of life. They have a definite psychological worth. Such factual incidents are usually without significance to the individual himself.

What happens here? The girl tells us more than once that she has hidden her head. She does not say so directly, but intimates that she has wanted to hide her head when she was a child. In itself that is an inconsequential remark. Why does she report it? She jumps from one fact to another, and one often receives the impression that one fact is supposed to justify the other. This is very common among neurotic people. They seek the most irrational justifications and proofs for the correctness of their conduct. They establish a private logic. They relate experiences which are quite ordinary, but to which they ascribe such importance that one thereupon wonders why so much weight is attached to them, until one discovers that these experiences or facts are supposed to be justifications. The psychic machinery of the neurotic is so delicate that its functioning is jarred by the slightest disturbance from the outside, and so it is protected with a cuirass of handy justifications. Nothing is permitted entry into the system until it is clubbed into form so that it fits.

We wonder at the dexterity of such a person who manipulates experiences and events until they fit into his style of life. If we did not know that the soul of man is a unity on which he works in order

THE CASE OF MISS R.

to arrange it more artistically, we should wonder why so insignificant a matter is projected. That is the compulsion of man's psychic life to unity, a part of the general creative power of the soul life.

I was accustomed to make my hats myself, usually from the remnants of the things father made. For the most part they were impossible, but sometimes one was wearable. The making of hats gradually became a mania. It went so far that father had to lock up all the extra pieces of material in the house.

I believe we have ascertained that she has a good visual sense. We can imagine that the joy of designing something pleasing to the eye stimulated her. To that we add that she has never been scolded, that everything she does or says is praised, and we can thus understand that hatmaking also represented a training. A deeper desire to create something pleasing so that she can shine, is obvious here.

Father had an old coat which he had promised to remodel for me. He never took the time off to do it. I became angry and scolded him. I believe, I said "bum" to him.

You know what friendly relations exist between her and her father, but you see how easily they can be broken when the question of power comes to the fore and when her father does not want to

THE SHOCK OF SEX KNOWLEDGE

follow her wish. It might be said that she is impulsive.

Impulsiveness is a question of temperament. What is temperament? Doctors, psychologists and philosophers all differ on the meaning of temperament. Since the days of the Greeks, temperament has been divided into four distinct classifications, the sanguine, the choleric, the melancholy and the phlegmatic. Such divisions are purely descriptive and merely made to satisfy the desire for order in human thought. Pure forms of temperament seldom occur; what we usually see are mixtures. A human being, during the course of his life, can also change from one temperament to another. The representatives of the natural sciences believe that temperaments are produced by the various activities of the inner glands, such as the thyroid gland, the sexual glands, the suprarenal glands and so on. This assumption is quite mechanical and has not been proved. We, on the contrary, regard the temperament as an expedient safety device, the development of which is determined by the degree of the feeling of inferiority and discouragement. Temperament is a means by which to attain one's fictive goal.

For centuries it has been supposed that temperament was inborn and inherited. That is one of those suppositions which serves to relieve us of responsibility. When a deed is ascribed to the temperament, the doer is no longer responsible. And even when

THE CASE OF MISS R.

bodily conditions (so-called dispositions) do have a certain amount of influence in the development of a certain temperamental quality, the objection may be raised that there is no bodily condition which compels an individual to assume a certain attitude toward life. There are, of course, specific physical conditions which suggest an abnormal attitude and make a normal one more difficult.

Temperament, like most mental qualities, is trained to serve as means to the attainment of the goal. He who believes he will achieve his object by being quiet and indolent, will become phlegmatic, but will remain phlegmatic only as long as it appears advantageous to him. He who believes he must storm ahead will become impulsive. Naturally the environment and the experiences as well as the physical constitution play an important but never compelling rôle in the formation and development of temperament. Every child is impulsive when she is so situated that she grows up as a pampered child and then has her wishes refused. Mention might be made of psychopathy, but she handles the matter quite correctly; we, with the same goal, would not act differently.

Father got up, gritted his teeth and struck me lightly. He didn't hurt me, but a little accident happened again because of my fear.

THE SHOCK OF SEX KNOWLEDGE

We may assume that this girl belongs to the physical type which loses control of the bladder in a condition of fear.

When the war came we had to knit all sorts of things for the soldiers, mittens, socks and so on. I had to knit a pair of mittens. I knit an index finger in the place of the thumb and vice versa and then I tried to stretch the fingers. When we had to deliver the knitted stuff, I was afraid to hand mine in, but luckily the teacher didn't notice anything.

Many worse things than that were handed out to the soldiers during the war.

I pitied the soldier who would get those mittens. . . . After an absence of two years Lina returned from Prague. She was quite elegant and had a lot of trunks with her. While she was unpacking, I got hold a pair of her shoes and tried them on. They fitted perfectly. They were the first ones with high heels I ever had on; father only allowed me shoes with low heels. Later when I was sent out to get some beer, I went quickly to the neighboring café. There were usually two men there one of whom had once asked me to play cards with him. I was a little in love with him.

It may astonish many of you that love is mentioned here. You are not certain whether it is love or

THE CASE OF MISS R.

whether the question of power does not play too great a rôle; it is possibly a relation which consists almost entirely of a striving for superiority. If this girl proceeds further, something will of a surety happen which will prevent the complete development of the affair.

He was there when I entered, but no matter how hard I tried to draw his attention to the high heels, he didn't notice them.

Something begins here to which one does not usually pay much heed—an attempt to make an impression. There is another striving underneath than the one usually considered, namely, the power motive.

Lina brought me some Bohemian slippers, a writing book and many other things which I do not remember. But when the perfume and liquid dentrifice appeared, I seized them and ran to rinse my mouth out, and sprayed my clothes with the perfume. Now we were all together again—that made me happy.

We know what makes her happy; the fulfillment of her desire for superiority. The more she approaches her ideal of being the center, the nearer she is to happiness. The bigger her court, the better.

We had a mouse in the house. When mother baked something, the mouse used to come through a crack

THE SHOCK OF SEX KNOWLEDGE

in the door. The smell attracted it. Mother and I were terribly afraid of mice.

It is very well known that girls dread and are disgusted by mice. There is a womanly motive in it, the motive of being taken by surprise, fear of being harmed by the mouse. It is not always a sexual symbol, but when you remember how girls act as soon as they hear of a mouse, how they protect themselves as if they were going to be assaulted, you can understand that it can be such a symbol in some cases.

I was sitting in my room and brooding. It was a habit of mine then.

The tendency of busying herself with useless things grows more marked.

Father carried the petroleum lamp to the kitchen and sat down at the sewing machine. And as I sat there in the shadow, something scurried across the floor from one side of the room to the other. I ran to father and cried, "a mouse!" Father was of the opinion that I was seeing mice everywhere and that it was only a moving shadow. . . . I had a good nose for the smell of a mouse.

We have already heard of her nose.

I could smell it distinctly on my music; I was always an extremely good smeller. One night, as so often happened, I was lying between my parents

157

THE CASE OF MISS R.

who were already asleep. It was dark and very quiet. I heard something breathing and scratching at the door. I was terror-stricken and thought at first it was a burglar. I drew the cover over my head and listened intently. Then I realized that it was a mouse and woke mother. Mother was not less frightened than I. Then I awakened father. He laughed at us. Jokingly I promised him a piece of silver if he would get out of bed and chase the mouse away. When he lit the lamp, the scratching ceased. Obviously the mouse was afraid of the light. . . . We bought a mousetrap, but it did not catch the mouse. The rodent became more and more impudent. We often heard it scratching in broad daylight. The mouse nauseated me so much that I tried to force my parents to move out. In order to quiet me, they used to tell the funniest mouse stories. They said that a mouse had once sprung into the pocket of our assistant, Krassny. Mother's brother liked to play with mice and once he even put one inside his shirt.

You see how the idea turns up that a mouse can hide itself in one's clothing in some way.

My dread could not be overcome. I couldn't eat another thing whenever I happened to hear the mouse scratching during mealtime. Finally mother borrowed another mousetrap from a neighbor, and we caught the mouse with it. Father wanted to drown

THE SHOCK OF SEX KNOWLEDGE

it; but when I saw it in the cage, it filled me with pity on account of its pleading eyes and troubled movements and I begged for its life.

How can we reconcile that with the girl's style of life? No matter how small this object is, she can now be the merciful one; she controls life and death. It gives her a feeling of strength. She will probably have her own way.

We went out into the street and let the mouse run free. . . . Soon after we caught a second mouse. But by that time I was so bitter that I agreed when they decided to drown it. Mother poured water into the pail; father took hold of the trap; I got up on the table to be safe. Unfortunately the mouse was too quick for them and sprang like a flash out of the trap and hid itself. Mother and I were furious. We knew that it would take care not to go into the trap again. A week later, when I came home one evening —our apartment was at the end of the house corridor—a mouse was sitting in front of our door.

She talks so much about mice that we are now attentive. There must be some connection with a former preparation for the sexual question; something is reflected there which has already been started.

I screamed, ran to the house door and shouted to my parents through the window for help.

THE CASE OF MISS R.

She behaves as she did when she saw the exhibitionist.

Mother immediately came out with a broom. The mouse had disappeared. It was doubtless the same one which we had already caught, and it did not dare, therefore, to enter our apartment. I believe it also warned the other mice about our house since, from that time on, we were spared any mice. I was also very much afraid, like. most other people, of rats. There were many in our courtyard. They used to creep out of the sewer pipe. Father often used to say that one could hear them whistling down the toilet pipe. When I heard that, I did not want to use the toilet any more. I was afraid that a rat could bite me when I sat down. We let the dog Bello hunt the rats. There was a wild scramble in the yard. The housekeeper with a broom, Bello, running after her, and all us children who were scared, but who ran around here and there. A mad mix-up. I also couldn't stand spiders.

She continues to list all the things she hated; she does not seem to emerge from this train of thought.

One morning when I was polishing my shoes, I felt something sticky in one of them. I thrust my hand inside and there was a partially crushed spider. I hurled the shoe in the corner and did not wear that pair for a long time. Once there was one on the wall

160

THE SHOCK OF SEX KNOWLEDGE

just above my bed. I sprang out of bed and called my parents. Father wanted to kill it. I was of the opinion, however, that that might mean bad luck and seized his arm. The spider finally landed in the pail.

One day Olga found in the trunk of her father, who had been in Siberia, . . .

A spider? A mouse? No.

. . . the memoirs of Casanova.

The close thought connection leads one to infer that a mouse was a sexual symbol in the life of this girl.

At that time I was in the third year of high school. We devoured the book. Then she discovered a lot of erotic books, bound in black, with the title, "The Secret Library," stamped in white. Trembling with excitement, we got the books out on the floor and read them aloud to each other. The books were called, "The Black Don Juan," "The Lady with the Dark Spot," "The Swimming Instructor in the Women's Bath," and so on. The most awful things happened in those stories.

It is natural that superficial observers will take this as an expression of eroticism. It is much more correct when it is understood as a divagation from eroticism, as an effort to give very little place in her

THE CASE OF MISS R.

real life to it. The reading of erotic descriptions indicated the exclusion of eroticism in reality.

I saw a postcard which fascinated me in the window of a stationery store. It depicted a centaur embracing a nymph in a suggestive fashion, while whispering something in her ear. I wanted very much to buy the card, but was ashamed. The picture troubled me constantly. Day after day it drew me to the store. Finally I made up my mind, entered the store and asked to be shown postcards. The one I wanted was among them. Full of joy I returned home and hid it among my underwear. And when I was alone, I would take it out, concentrate on it, imagining myself sometimes the centaur and sometimes the nymph.

While we formerly found that she sought sexual excitement in her reading, she goes further here and begins to interest herself in pictures. She goes over into the visual.

The postcard made no impression on Olga.

One may conclude from that, that they go different ways in their erotic development. Olga is another type; possibly she is not so frightened.

Funny that boys could not attract me when I thought they were superior.

Here we find a corroboration of the reason given

THE SHOCK OF SEX KNOWLEDGE

for examining pictures and reading erotic books. She shuns love in that she occupies her fantasy with useless things. Boys are only there to be made fools of.

When we depreciate the value of something which we originally wanted, we rid ourselves of a disagreeable duty or responsibility, and retain our good humor. That is also the meaning of the fable of the fox and sour grapes. When the fox saw he could not reach the grapes, he consoled himself by saying they were sour, and thereby retained his good humor.

I never kissed one. The love life of my youth existed in fantasies. I used to imagine the story of King Saul in which he sent the husband of the woman he loved to war. And again that a woman was stolen by a knight, raped and her husband pursued by servants. There always had to be a broken marriage.

You remember that she has already had sexual fantasies.

Gradually erotic images no longer satisfied me, and I went about making them visible. I drew on a piece of paper a woman with a voluptuous figure, and a strong man, cut out the figures and laid them together so that they embraced. But I was a bad artist and my silhouettes looked awful. Therefore I decided to write a story.

A new training begins at this point, or it is the continuation of one already begun which is to be

163

THE CASE OF MISS R.

taken as a preparation for her life story. She writes skillfully and fluently.

I first composed an introduction which told of a blond, immaculate girl and her betrothed. I described the person of the girl in detail; the man interested me less. Then the novel began. I let a friend of the fiancé appear, an untrustworthy fellow who immediately desired the girl. And she who treated her lover badly fell in love with the brutal friend. In a scene where the friend, from a hiding place, watches the girl bathing, I described her again in minute detail and was fascinated by my own description.

Here also those who have some understanding of human nature can recognize this deviation and how she searches for a new road in order to escape the normal in eroticism. Here you see how this aberration is nothing but the shoddy rest which remains when the normal is excluded.

At the end I described an embrace between them. . . . I loved to watch myself in the mirror.

We see the predisposition to the visual. Such girls who remind one of the voyeur type are always strongly attracted by mirrors.

Other girls disgusted me.

That is an attempt not to proceed further in the direction of homosexuality.

THE SHOCK OF SEX KNOWLEDGE

My own person pleased me most. . . . At that time I was in low spirits and went around with bowed head, not daring to look people in the face, imagined every one could see through me and was afraid I wouldn't grow any more. I was horribly unhappy. Finally I went to father and whispered to him, "I have a confession to make." He asked me what was the matter now.

This sort of question is heard only in connection with spoiled children. They occupy one the whole day long.

And I confessed with shame that I had done a certain thing. He said it didn't matter once, but I had better not do it again or I would harm myself.

She has found a more advanced road in eroticism; she has arrived at auto-eroticism. We can predict, in accordance with the girl's style of life, that she will cling to it for a long time. This satisfaction offers her several advantages. First she derives physical pleasure. This pleasure is not only harmless, producible at will, but carries with it no binding consequences. Tense emotions which might force her to solve her love problem in more realistic fashion, are thereby released. The problem of love is circumvented. The question of power is solved to her satisfaction since she threatens her father with the possibility of a sordid habit and is unassailable. Re-

THE CASE OF MISS R.

tention of the habit over a long period is a sign of an asocial attitude. It is the eroticism of the lonely.

Now I felt better. But on the next day I began again. And every time I did it, I would go and confess to father.

It is to be explained why she did not hide it. She has her father in her power; she will force him to watch her more closely. She has secured a further protection for herself and given her father something else to do. He must watch so that she does not repeat it.

They used to watch me in bed, but in bed nothing happened.

CHAPTER IX

THE MASCULINE PROTEST

*W*HEN *I was fourteen, I resumed my swearing at my parents and at God.*

We must assume that difficulties have entered the life of the girl as they come across the path of every spoiled child. It is impossible to continue such pampering forever and this swearing means nothing other than anger at the deprivation expressed in degrading remarks.

The pampered child struggles for the continuation of the pampering. One can give the word "pampering" various meanings and say, "I understand this or that by pampering." But that is a waste of time. The moment she believes she is not being sufficiently pampered, she attempts in her rage to degrade the others. For herself at least, the child is in the foreground and overrides the others. Scolding is an attempt to degrade others. With the exception of very few children, every child has gone through some phase of being spoiled. This phase is present in the style of life. The interest in favorable situations is

167

THE CASE OF MISS R.

sharpened. The chief concern lies in the endeavor to regain the pampering. The trait to dominate, to tyrannize, is developed. It is apparent that scolding which is directed toward stronger persons and God cannot be separated from the feeling of one's own superiority.

(Case: A girl who had an illicit love relation suffered from the fixed idea that every one was a murderer. She was the oldest child, spoiled, ambitious, and brought up by her grandmother. When we hear the word grandmother, we can predict the pampering. When she was sixteen, she began an affair with an older man. That signifies weakness and a desire to be pampered. The saying goes "An old man's darling." The affair lasted a long time and is explained thus: I am stubborn and want to have my own way, and this man is also stubborn so we have decided not to marry. That is the logic of the neurotic. The man was good, gave in to her in almost everything and withheld his approval of only one thing—her cooking. The girl took particular exception to this. One day this girl witnessed a murder in the neighborhood. That was a terrifying fact for her. It made a deep impression upon her. She used the word as a condemnation of civilization in order to degrade every one and everything so that, as a consequence, she seemed to herself to be the only pure and innocent one left. We shall see how and why she does it.

THE MASCULINE PROTEST

Her lover had avoided introducing her to his family, and she could not endure it. We could have predicted that she would not be able to endure a free love relationship. She would feel herself confined and protest vigorously. During the war her lover was sick and she went to much trouble to provide milk for him. When she finally had procured some milk his mother took it from her but then shut the door in her face. This girl was in a situation in which she valued the man because she needed him. The love relationship had much more significance for her than for a balanced person. She wanted to be ahead of every one and wanted to put her own will through with force. She preferred the continuation of the relationship but there was something offensive about it. She achieved a certain measure of freedom for herself when she cursed persons whom she did not know. We can compare this conflict somewhat with the feminine gesture which is directed against the disadvantage falling to the lot of the female sex (the masculine protest). She did not get so far—she reached only resentment and anger. She revenged herself in that she looked upon every respectable person as a murderer; that means a condemnation of our culture. In the beginning she condemned herself with the rest, later she excluded herself. Thus she was a saint and every one else a devil.)

Without moving my lips, the most abominable

THE CASE OF MISS R.

words used to enter my mind. I felt terribly depressed.

Depression is often found with a compulsion neurosis. A depression often starts when an individual believes that he is forced by some power to pursue a certain course of action. Since such courses of action are almost sure to obstruct somewhat the activities of others or, at least, to prevent one from being occupied with useful things, the resulting depression resembles a self-accusation and self-reproach and is taken as such. Often the depression is expressed by a self-conviction. But this self-conviction has another meaning, and one should not be fooled by it. We want to study how depression fits into the system of this girl and we shall therefore make some comments on depression in general.

Depression is a weapon used to elevate one's own position. The necessity for help from strangers is demonstrated through weakness, tears, sad moods and complaining, and other persons are forced into service. Depression is related to melancholy, a miniature of it, so to speak.

An individual who fears a failure in life, or whom failure has overtaken, can point to depression or melancholy as the reason for the failure, and thereby free himself of responsibility, in that he himself demonstrates his own weakness and need for help. The neurotic logic thus finds a justification for domineer-

THE MASCULINE PROTEST

ing over others. Insufficient social activity in youth sometimes results in the peculiarly aggressive attitude of depressed or melancholy people, which can be compared to partial suicide in that one damages oneself and threatens revenge on the environment. When a depressed person reproaches himself, he reveals an exaggerated notion of his own importance. In addition, there is always to be detected a complaint that it is partly, if not altogether, the fault of others. Supported by this grumbling, the subordination and assistance of the others is demanded and one's own irresponsibility and superiority realized. Depressions grow out of a suspicious and harshly critical attitude toward society and are usually developed in early youth.

We can see in a general description of the depressed mood the same characteristics which the writer of this life story reveals; the manifest striving over and control of her environment to make firm her own security. Her system does not prefer primarily to rule through weakness. She will use this means only when she cannot succeed with a direct aggression or when she has gone too far and is forced to apply the brakes. Here she needs the depression in order to have a justifiable burden. The feeling of being heavily borne down she exaggerates thus: "I fight against it but cannot rid myself of it. To be forced to do or say things is a terrible burden."

THE CASE OF MISS R.

And often I was at the point of confessing to my father.

She has the tendency to make her father her confidant; she wants to indicate to him: "I am so unhappy, one must give in to me, every one must let himself be dominated by me."

I couldn't bring myself to do it. It was the only thing I kept secret from him. I felt miserable.

Even if she doesn't tell her father anything, he will notice the change soon enough. She will attract his attention through her ill appearance, her sickly and absent-minded manner.

And when I saw him before me with his weak arms, it hurt me dreadfully. I thought, "If he only knew."

She feels herself superior through her degradation of him. His weak arms!

I tried in vain to convince myself that I meant some one else when I thought of a bad name.

She wants to feel noble.

Then came the thought in between, "Father is a . . ." In order to prove to myself that father was not a . . . I thought, "Father is not a . . . ; his assistant is a . . . ," and cried, "He can go to the devil." Then I kept still and heard within me again

THE MASCULINE PROTEST

"Father is a . . ." Then it seemed to me as if all my cursing were aimed at father, and I felt as if some one had hit me a hard blow on the head.

When we ask ourselves whether some one can demand anything from the girl, we have to answer this question in the negative. She busies herself constantly with useless things and lets all her energy be consumed by them. She has no confidence in herself. Her attitude expresses her doubts whether she will have such a position in life as she has now in her family, and whether she will be able to solve her problems so that she can always remain in the center of the stage.

Her neurosis begins at this point. When we look back, we become aware of the prolonged preparation which has consistently led to this point. Her entire behavior tends toward an evasion of the duties of a normal life in the society of her fellow human beings. She fills her time instead by occupying herself constantly with the matter of superiority in her own circle. When her superiority is endangered, and the problems of life approach more and more closely, the first compulsion symptoms appear. She curses her family and God. She has practiced this as a child. We can now definitely determine that she is on the road to a neurosis. Her exaggerated desire for superiority and what we have termed her hesitating attitude have indicated this development for some

THE CASE OF MISS R.

time. There can scarcely remain any doubt that she will sink more and more deeply into the mire of neurotic thought and behavior. In the vicious circle of a neurosis, a neurotic act provokes a strong reaction which calls forth a still stronger act in the same false direction, which thereupon arouses a still stronger reaction, and so on. In general it is impossible for a neurotic to find his way alone out of the labyrinth of his neurosis. Because of the patient's lack of penetrating understanding and his obsession for power, it is almost impossible to effect an improvement without some outside, objectively comprehensive assistance.

It will be instructive to follow the advancement of this compulsion neurosis. I should like to explain in more detail the character of a compulsion neurosis to prepare a better understanding of this girl's story.

Compulsion neuroses are those forms of neurosis in which certain compulsion symptoms, such as compulsion-washing, praying, brooding, etc., govern an individual's life. These compulsions work like commands, disobedience of which, according to the patient's arguments, would be followed by the direst consequences. Such compulsion symptoms torment the person who has them and arouse in him an anxious, painful mood.

When we observe what really happens (as we always do in individual psychology) what the patient

THE MASCULINE PROTEST

achieves with his symptoms, the meaning of a compulsion becomes clear. The compulsion neurotic has approached life's demands pretty closely. All the more complete and demonstrative is his retreat. Like all neurotics he is ambitious, but discouraged. When there comes an imagined difficulty which he does not have sufficient courage to tackle, he shoves between himself and this difficulty a barrier constructed by his teetering ambition, and this barrier assumes the character of a compulsion. He piles up a mountain of obstacles in front of him like a mountain of refuse, and when life demands something of him, he excuses himself by pointing to the refuse heap. He seems to be using up all his energy to overcome this mountain which he has himself built, but what he really does is avoid the problem or demand. The diligence and haste with which he works, the severity and ostensible inevitableness of his compulsion, are supposed to legitimatize his good intention.

In his attempt to combat the symptom, the patient assumes the right to produce it and, arguing according to his own private logic, becomes at the same time judge, complainant and defendant.

As in all neuroses, the goal of a compulsion neurosis is superiority. We claim that the neurosis (including the compulsion neurosis) is an illness of *position* and not of *disposition*. The compulsion neurotic substitutes his own compulsion for the compulsion of the

THE CASE OF MISS R.

world upon him. His own self-elevation and lust for power is mirrored in the substitute compulsion. The main reason for and probably the main purpose of the arrangement of a compulsion neurosis is the frittering away of time which protects him from the necessity of solving, or even making an attempt to solve his problems. Only when we look ahead to the goal and result of a neurosis, can we understand the sense of it. The outbreak of a compulsion neurosis prevents, like a revolt, a yielding to the demands of communal life. That is the purpose.

The objection may be raised that the patient may very well be satisfied and happy with the superiority which he wins, and with the certainty with which he protects himself from the imagined danger of facing his problems. This would indeed be so, were it not a seeming superiority, a seeming certainty. A patient does not construct a neurosis by purely intellectual means; he brings to his aid his entire being, all his abilities and feelings in the arrangement of this yes-but mode of life. The neurosis is a weapon, a club; that is to say, the neurotic believes himself to be surrounded by enemies against whom he must fight till he has secured that which he considers the booty of victory. There is no room, under such circumstances, for joyous feelings which would hinder him in fulfilling his intentions. He must pay dearly for the waste heap he piles up.

THE MASCULINE PROTEST

If we apply this general explanation to the life story of our young girl, we see her energetically occupied in establishing between herself and the community a barrier, a waste heap. She feels herself compelled to curse God and her relatives, reproaches herself when she is depressed, rules her environment and wastes her time with useless things. Like every neurotic, she uses her neurosis in order to be able to say: I have not been able to solve my life problems, because I have been so overburdened with these things. This "because" is typical. It is the neurotic justification in a special logic which is arranged to evade the true logic of life and to fit the patient's needs. Every person with some common sense can see how weak this justification is. And yet the neurotic must believe in it as he believes in something holy, whereby he gives one to understand that in him is some glimmering of the distance between his conduct and the real demands of communal life. Otherwise why should he have to justify himself?

I was never safe from the compulsion of swearing in the street or in company.

We see how she answers the first question of life (social contact). She creates a great distance between herself and others. Her swearing prevents contact with other persons.

I was even afraid of myself. I was always worried

177

THE CASE OF MISS R.

lest some accident happen to me to punish me.

Here one can see what the feeling of guilt really intends. Its only purpose is to increase the waste heap upon which it is thrown. Nietzsche is right when he says "Conscience pricks are indecent."

I endeavored to distract myself by every means possible.

We know in advance that she will not be successful.

Once when Minna and I were returning from the gymnasium I talked continually in order to drown my thoughts. Suddenly I choked, had to stop and listen. . . . Once I saw a criminal film, "The Man with Nine Fingers." It was horrible. An old woman was murdered in the film. My parents awaited me after the performance. My father said it was poison for me, but he did not divine the principal cause of my excitement. I seemed to myself like the murderer of my parents. In my thoughts I also had to swear at God. And then I heard a shriek as if it were from a devil, "You, you have said all that." Inwardly I answered at once: "God is the most beautiful man, and the best one there is." While I was saying "Our Father," I heard "Holy Mary, I pray to thee. No, I don't pray to thee."

There you have a pretty picture. When one moves

THE MASCULINE PROTEST

to the left and then to the right nothing happens; it looks as if one had done something, and while one wastes one's time thus, time goes on and one avoids solving problems.

Then there was an inward whisper again: "I pray to thee, Maria." I was perspiring with fear.

Such fixed ideas must shatter their thinker. In this shattering lies the principal purpose of the neurosis. Now we understand the significance of feelings a little better. Feelings are never arguments, they run in the direction demanded by the individual style of life. We can go a step further; the arrangement works toward the goal of producing such feelings as will lighten the task of the neurotic to obey (follow) his style of life. This girl helps herself in that she produces feelings which build themselves into an impassable barrier for her. We hear that she does not want to go out into society, we hear that she does not train for a vocation, and we hear that she will fail in the third test imposed by life, in the matter of love.

Then the swearing used to proceed with full force. I would have to start praying again. I tried with all my strength but the nasty thoughts would come in between—it often took an hour before I could finish a prayer.

She has no connection with religion.

THE CASE OF MISS R.

At that time I began to interest myself in men.

God helps the righteous.

I wanted to please all. I received compliments about my eyes and paid special attention to them.

Other psychologists would be happy. She is beginning to flirt a bit. We know that she will remain where she is.

I took some trouble to protect my eyes so that they would not lose in lustre.

A new occupation. Another compulsion.

Sometimes I used to take a neighbor's little girl in her carriage to the park.

She would prefer to be in the child's carriage herself with someone else pushing her. We know that that will have a bad end.

It was very sunny there. I became apprehensive that the sun might dazzle my sight.

Refer to Freud's monograph on a paranoiac. If that is not a new hindrance, then there is no hindrance at all in the soul.

From that moment I avoided the sun.

She protects her eyes. Many psychologists would say it was a sign that she wants to find a man, and

THE MASCULINE PROTEST

would not notice that one can change something into the opposite. One can protect one's eyes to the point where there are no men at all.

When you want to illuminate such vague symptoms then you must approach them with the individual psychological question: What happens when a girl like this attempts to avoid the sun? All attachments are obviated by it, especially love, from which she draws further and further away.

I used to watch anxiously lest a ray of sunlight fall on me. I avoided all sunny spots. When I was forced to leave the shadow . . .

You see how much she has to occupy herself with it.

. . . and accidentally raised my head in the sun, I would talk it into myself that I had been dazzled by the sun.

When one glances back at the superstitions of peoples, at the mythological details where there is talk of similar things, one can discern the marvellous phantom of the ancients. Even in Hamlet there is a warning to women not to go into the sun or a pregnancy may follow. That comes from an old superstition.

However, we do not have to assume that archaic thoughts were behind the girl's phantoms; it is suf-

THE CASE OF MISS R.

ficient when she has found something whereby she is cut off from the problem which she seeks to avoid.

I thought it out thus, that the sun had taken away some of my power of sight, and that I would have to go blind. Day by day this thought came to me. Consciousness of the fact that I saw as well as ever was lacking.

She would have been able to do nothing with such insight; it would not have helped her system. Only when she imagines that she has been harmed, can she withdraw—that is to say, escape—the solution of life's problems.

When Lina went out with me, I begged her to avoid the sun. I wanted to find out if she trusted herself in the sun. She laughed and declined to follow this procedure. Then mother came along. That didn't satisfy me at all.

You see how she hardens herself and that common sense is no longer of help. He who asks the naïve question, "Why are common sense grounds of no more use?" overlooks the fact that she does not behave sensibly but wants to run away. You can describe the wonder of the thundering guns at the front to a deserter a hundred times, but he will only permit himself those trains of thought which help him to flee.

THE MASCULINE PROTEST

I used to get hold of Olga or some other friend and make her look at the sun.

That is her unsocial trait. She is possessed by the idea that the power of sight is weakened by the sun and permits all others to look at the sun.

So that they would not think I had become a fool I arranged it so that they noticed nothing. For example, I said: "I don't know what is in my eye, I can't look at the sun, can you?" And as soon as one raised her eyes to the sun I had to laugh uproariously.

That looks as if she were purposely trying to do harm, as if she thought it desirable that the others should have their sight weakened. It is the laugh of the victor, probably an attempt to be bodily superior to the others, supported by the idea that she knows a secret. She is superior for the others do not know it.

I was of the opinion that their eyes were dazzled by it and that made me glad.

You see how that is again confirmed.

I always had my eyes cast down on the street. When I raised my eyes I always protected them with my hand. In spite of my precautions, however, the idea pursued me. Then I would run home like one possessed and say to my father, weeping: "I have been

THE CASE OF MISS R.

dazzled by the sun. I'm disgusted with everything, I'm going to kill myself."

She pushes her desertion to the extreme and plays with thoughts of suicide. She has lost hope. Arms, legs, eyes have lost their appeal.

Then I complained bitterly to my parents because they wanted to let me go away. At first they laughed and asked whether I had gone crazy. Father assured me that the sun had great healing power. He often went to the window, opened it, and cried to me, "Look here, how I open my eyes in the sun. I should be glad if I could go walking in the sun every day." When I saw how father let the sun shine on him I became confused. Then I began to lament all over again. . . . I had a feeling of anxiety continuously, as if I was always sensing a terrible danger.

This danger is, of course, a defeat in love as we have found up to now. She is too proud. A girl who wants to be ahead of every one cannot reconcile herself to the idea that she can meet defeat and so her anxiety is concretized.

Finally I hardly dared to go out on the street. I was also afraid that a stroke of lightning could hit and dazzle me. If the sun barely shone through a window on me, or if someone played with a mirror and the reflected light passed over me I was terror-stricken.

THE MASCULINE PROTEST

Don't go in the sun. Let no one see you, you cannot compete.

Nowhere did I feel safe. I said to myself that the accident which was fated to happen to one was inescapable, even if one locked oneself in a room. I was already sick of life and wondered, if things did not improve with me, whether it would be better to kill myself instead of going on to meet such a fate.

And now there are consequences to this idea. She pushes the problem of seeing in the foreground. In order to justify this attitude she had to find other measures. So we hear:

In order not to strain my eyes I read as little as possible.

We are reminded here that she has spoken with emphasis of reading salacious books. This can be a withdrawal from them and a confirmation that she must protect her eyes.

When I read I was always annoyed by being able to see the tip of my nose.

We can understand that very well because she was always looking at the tip of her nose. That would hold good for others too, but others have no interest in the matter. It is a very good excuse for eliminating reading.

185

THE CASE OF MISS R.

I talked it into myself . . .

We are approaching a beauty defect.

. . . that I was cross-eyed. I turned myself here and there, held the book in different positions—the tip of the nose followed me like a bad conscience.

You see how she preoccupies herself more and more with things which make it possible for her to think that her eyes are weakening. We ask ourselves rightly what still remains when her eyes are gone.

I once read in the Bible that some dirt was blown into the eyes of a saint and that he became blind. This I now recalled. Dirt meant to me bird dung. And I watched carefully when I passed a tree. I also tried to avoid drain pipes where the sparrows and pigeons gathered. I used to look much at green lawns and bushes because I had heard that green was good for the eyes.

The more tricks she conjures up to strengthen her eyes the more her conviction grows that the condition of her eyes is bad.

If the lampshade was not put on the petroleum lamp I would become absolutely mad with rage.

You see how this tendency overhauls her lust for power so that the others must follow her wishes.

THE MASCULINE PROTEST

I never looked at light or fire. Here and there people talked of diseases of the eye, for example, of cataract. When they talked they pointed to their eyes. I strictly avoided doing that. When I noticed that I had done it unknowingly I was at once afraid that I would get the disease of which they were then speaking.

That is one of the usual marks of hypochondriacs or compulsion neurotics. They take up everything which they can possibly fit into the neurotic mess in order to fritter away the time, in order to gain protection, security against being dragged into the life stream. They feel the stream of life and hang on to their neurotic straps.

I imagined that the eyes could jump out of the sockets as a result of straining them. I pressed them back carefully with my fingers.

One is astonished at the ostensible nonsense. This girl is possessed by the thought: how can I protect myself, secure myself from having to accept love, marriage, the rôle of a woman? She is indifferent to everything else and feels safe. Behind this confusion a star shines dimly—released from the rôle of a woman. She pays the price, she suffers, but only to get her reward in the future.

I refused to let a blind piano tuner come to the house. It seemed to me that blindness might be con-

187

THE CASE OF MISS R.

tagious. Often I even imagined that I had bumped my eyes against something and they had been knocked out. This delusion lasted for three months and was followed by a disturbance again started by a compliment.

Compliments were paid to her eyes so she attempted to destroy them.

This time it was my teeth with which my disordered imagination began to busy itself.

Someone has complimented her on her teeth; that means, you are fit, though, for the rôle of a woman.

I was drinking from a glass and struck the glass against the edge of one of my upper front teeth. I suddenly imagined that I had broken off a piece of the tooth. I ran anxiously to father and cried; "For God's sake! Have I broken off a piece of my tooth?"

Again exit beauty!

Then I opened my mouth and let father look inside. "Where?" he asked, astonished. In order to see whether he could find the damaged tooth himself I didn't tell him which one I thought I had hurt. But when he could find nothing I cried, "A front tooth," and pointed to the one. Mother and father examined the tooth carefully, from all sides, and could not discover a scratch. I became angrier, ran to the mirror and looked at it myself.

THE MASCULINE PROTEST

Picture this girl: a compliment to her eyes works like a call to go to the front of life. Now a compliment has been paid her teeth and she is going to attack them.

And it seemed to me that it was a shade shorter than the adjoining tooth. So now I was quite convinced that I had broken off a piece and began to cry wretchedly. When Lina came home . . .

You remember that she is a professional, being a dentist's assistant.

. . . she had to look into my mouth. She could find nothing. I asked her if she would dare to strike a glass against her teeth. She laughed, took a glass and tapped her teeth with it. I stood there and watched her earnestly. I had always been very particular about my teeth. I remember the following:

This is the tooth complex. She will now prove that everything was not always as it should have been with her teeth.

The front milk teeth were very shaky. It would have been necessary to tug only slightly at them to have pulled them out. Father wanted to try it with a string. I preferred to try it myself, tied a piece of thread around a tooth, made the other end fast to the door knob and began to pull carefully. I became afraid and let the thing go. Then a dentist who

189

THE CASE OF MISS R.

was a friend of the family looked at my teeth. I opened my mouth unwillingly. And before I knew what was happening the tooth which was shakiest was already out. But he let the tooth fall in my mouth and in my excitement I swallowed it. My parents were very much exercised. For a few days I had to eat cabbage. When I was six one of my teeth hurt. On the way to the dentist I cried and complained and didn't want to go. Father promised me a pocketbook if I permitted the dentist to pull out the tooth. I wanted the pocketbook first and father really bought me a very pretty bag. Then he advised me to think of the brave "Tin Soldier" and everything he had had to go through. When we got to the dentist's house I halted for a moment in front of his door, and then said to father "Let's go to another—I'll surely cry with this one, and with another I'll have more courage." We turned around and went to another. He looked at the aching tooth and advised pulling it. I whispered to my father: "I have to consider it—he has such an angry face—let's go to another." And with some excuse or other we left him and finally returned home. I got such an awful toothache that night, however, that mother had to go with me the first thing the next morning to the dentist. I concentrated on the "Tin Soldier" and finally let the tooth be pulled.

But that was long ago. Now I had my anxiety

THE MASCULINE PROTEST

about my teeth without any visible reason, without any pain. The idea alone that I might, in some way, strike my mouth against some object, was enough to make me think I had knocked a tooth out. When the idea occurred to me, I always used to consider the position in which I found myself at the moment and measure the distance between me and the nearest object, such as a box or the piano. I wanted to prove to myself that it was impossible for me to have hit myself against it. I had retained that much sense. But the only result of this proof was that I became still more excited. For then I believed I had not taken enough care and had really damaged a tooth. And then I would measure distances again. And then I would again imagine that I had broken a tooth or at least scratched one. I experimented so long until I was exhausted by my efforts and excitement. And finally, quite discouraged, I would upbraid myself: "How can a person be so stupid as to knock out a tooth on purpose?"

Now she imagines that she has already knocked one out. A tooth plays an extraordinarily important part. I do not doubt that one can see the way by which a person arrives at a tooth-fetishism. Her tooth-complex is not fully developed, but one cannot deny that a tooth is greatly overvalued by her.

My parents had to look into my mouth constantly.

THE CASE OF MISS R.

You see how the wasting of time grows to undue proportions and how she becomes the center of the family.

Naturally they never found anything. No one could find the slightest thing the matter, not even I. I didn't believe the others or myself.

She helps herself quite simply in order to be able to go further. She is concerned with her teeth and not with her duties as a woman.

And so when I discovered tiny irregularities in my teeth which I had not noticed before, I imagined they were the damages I had inflicted on myself and began again to fume. Sometimes when I was eating cherries it happened that I bit on a cherry stone. That depressed me to such an extent and drove me into such a condition that I needed a whole day in which to recover. Finally I used to squeeze the pits out of the cherries before I ate the fruit. I even had a peculiar way of eating apples. I cut them in thin slices, laid a slice at a time on the knife, and inserted the knife carefully into my mouth. Once the knife struck against my teeth and I immediately thought I had bitten on the knife. I was beside myself and shrieked: "No one has ever done that before, to bite on a knife and break one's teeth off." My parents demanded to know what the matter was now. Lina happened to be there. Everyone was amused as if glad at what

192

THE MASCULINE PROTEST

had happened. Father was of the opinion that I deserved it, what with my exaggerated carefulness. I became still more excited, thought father really meant that I had broken off my teeth and that by my own fault. Chokingly I cried: "Now you do admit that I have knocked out my teeth?" Father rejoined, "I don't admit anything. But when you are so stupid as to imagine anything like that it's about time you ate apples like all other persons." I did not stop crying. Lina picked up a knife and tapped her teeth with it. Then she asked me smilingly if the performance were sufficient. Little by little I became quieter. About two months later I noticed that there was some tartar on my teeth. I had scratched it off before with a needle. When I remembered that, I became terribly unhappy. "My God!" I said to myself, "certainly no one does that—scratch the enamel off one's teeth." I wanted to commit suicide. When I drank coffee I used to think that the heat of the coffee might crack the enamel. I refused to drink anything too hot or too cold, and drank coffee, tea, soup, beer, even water, lukewarm. I ate nothing hard. I was afraid to break a tooth if I did. I ate no more bread crusts, no meat in which there was a bone. No chocolate and no sugar. Then I didn't chew anything any more. I let the foods melt in my mouth and then swallowed them like a toothless hag. That looked so funny that my parents used to laugh until

THE CASE OF MISS R.

they cried. Then I avoided even bringing an eating utensil in contact with my teeth. I opened my mouth as wide as possible and inserted the food as carefully as I could or sucked the food up from the spoon or plate. Finally I ate only with my fingers. In the tram, when a window rattled, I became anxious and thought it might fall and knock out a tooth.

You will observe that she arranges her life so that she is freed from every occupation.

This delusion also lasted several months. But a still worse one followed. I had an excruciating youth.

I was just returning from school. I had accompanied a friend and wanted to cross the street. A man approached us from the other side. He had a cloth around his face. I thought at first he had a toothache. When he came nearer I noticed that his whole face was eaten away. There was no nose, no lips, only a number of red holes. I felt as if some one had struck me. I was seized with such dread of this man that in order not to retrace his footsteps I turned around and made a detour home.

Now comes the lupus phobia * and brings with it the fear of infection. We now see more clearly and can prophesy that this fear of infection will lead her to strengthen her feeling of security and support her still more in her attempt to exclude love and marriage from her life.

* Fear of lupus, which is a tuberculosis of the skin.

CHAPTER X

A LUPUS PHOBIA

THE last thing she collected in her effort to rid herself of reality was a man with a rash.

I was seized with such dread of this man, that in order not to retrace his footsteps, I turned around and made a detour home.

You see how the impact of these impressions which are to drive her further and further away from life is intensified. Again and again she finds an excuse for continuing her flight.

Still extremely frightened I told father what had happened.

It is striking that she tells it to her father and one may well ask why. The obvious answer would be that she is on good terms with him and has confidence in him. But we can find another reason in her behavior: she wants to make him understand what is going to follow—that she must attach herself still more closely to her family, lessen her contact with the outside world, appear laden with burdens and in-

THE CASE OF MISS R.

capable of doing anything or of solving any problems.

He thought it was probably lupus. What was that? A devouring disease whose name in Latin means wolf.

The father, who had a morbid fear of tuberculosis, had two or three medical books which he often read —hence his knowledge. It might be said that the father also has a phobia, and that she has therefore inherited his fear. But it is not so. The girl trains herself. She takes the means which she can use and which appear serviceable to her in the specific situation—whether from father or elsewhere. Supported by her fear of an infectious disease, she now believes she has the right to separate herself from the outside world. Why should that be an inherited trait? She wants to be at the top and observes that it is impossible for her to attain in the outside world the favorable, central place she occupies in the bosom of her family. We should like to ask of him who doubts this: who would leave a favorable situation in order to put himself into an unfavorable one? Common sense speaks here and profound hypotheses are not in place. If some one wishes to object, he has first to show us whether he would willingly leave an agreeable situation to enter a disagreeable one.

I wanted to know if this disease was infectious.

A LUPUS PHOBIA

I have already indicated that it is not impossible that this girl already knows something of infectious diseases of the sex organs.

He assured me that it was not the case. But I did not believe him. Not even when Lina confirmed his words. From the very beginning I was firmly convinced that lupus was infectious.

I should like to add a word about the peculiar methods of the nervous when they establish their conceptions. They must be right, and everything is turned about until they have proved what they set out to prove. This disease must be infectious. Even if all authorities were to say it was not she would still assert it was. You find with almost every neurosis this false logic whose force lies in the fact that it permits the patient to do what she otherwise would do without proof. For example, I knew a patient who had always played the leading rôle in her family and whose situation suddenly became unfavorable through an unsuccessful marriage. She arranged a hunger strike, explained that she could eat nothing because she had a weak lung and got an attack of coughing when she had to swallow the food, and harmed her lung thereby. That is an attempt at suicide. When such a patient gets to the point where she asserts that the most important thing at the moment is to get up and go for a walk in order to stimulate

THE CASE OF MISS R.

her appetite, she arranges matters so that the conditions are impossible of fulfillment and so that her insight will not interfere with her neurotic striving. A "no" in answer to life is clear.

Even though two persons who know about it insist that lupus is not infectious she is not to be convinced.

I should have preferred never to set foot again on that street. But we lived just around the corner, and the way to school was through it, so I could not avoid it. Gradually this fear vanished.

How are we to explain this? You hear that such a disorder can only disappear when it is treated by way of psychological interpretation. Symptoms of illness as the outer, visible signs of a neurosis are labile and vanish for a time, or sometimes change into other symptoms without psychological treatment. The patient is always endeavoring to adjust himself to the varying pressure exerted upon him by his environment. The girl says; *Gradually this fear disappeared of itself.* If we were of the opinion that her symptom was of sexual origin (repressed libidinous wishes, for instance) then we would have to assume that her libido has undergone a transformation. Such an interpretation is too far-fetched and, in addition, false. We know that she has temporarily lost her courage. As soon as she regains it in some measure, her ma-

A LUPUS PHOBIA

chinations are felt to be superfluous and she tries once more to find a way to life. It is self-evident that when her courage increases a little she loses her anxiety. We see the hesitating attitude of this girl toward the question of love. We observe how she seeks to escape it. We want to have further confirmation as to whether we are on the right road. All these phases are nothing other than attempts to escape a solution to the question of love.

One afternoon a boy called for me, an acquaintance of Olga's, who was attentive to both of us. We went for a walk together and happened to pass a street where there was a home for people suffering from lupus. The windows of the home were covered with green netting similar to the netting of which one makes nets to catch butterflies. I heard the whirring sound of some apparatus. All at once I noticed where we were. I was horribly depressed, spoke not another word and turned to go home completely broken. I was as if lamed. My thoughts stood still and only one thing filled me—dread of lupus.

Just at the time when she is with the boy who is attentive to two girls something fills her with dread. There are two reasons in explanation: (1) that the boy also likes another girl; (2) that she can use her lupus phobia to escape the solution of any problem.

THE CASE OF MISS R.

At first I could not answer at all the worried questions of my parents as to why I was so upset. Horrible thoughts whirled in my head. I thought that the people who accidentally trod in the footsteps of a lupus sufferer would spread the germs over the whole city.

Now the whole town is full of lupus. Now she cannot go anywhere any more. The distance between her and the question of love grows step by step.

"Where," I asked myself, "is there a place on earth where there is no lupus? Where is there a spot where no lupus sufferer has left bacteria behind him?" The whole world appeared to me infected.

You see here the gesture of exclusion of the spoiled child.

I felt as if I were surrounded by bars through which there was no way out. At the same time I felt I hated and loathed the lupus sufferers.

At this point we shall also pause a moment. Most people would say that that was a natural and understandable gesture of rejection. But there are other situations in the life of a neurotic person where the same gesture appears without its being natural and understandable. For example, what does an exaggerated fear of mice or spiders signify? Why does a nervous individual emphasize his hate and loathing

A LUPUS PHOBIA

so forcibly? There is no logical ground for it. The gesture demonstrates a feeling and aims at something other than an imaginary fear. In our case it serves as a means to preserve the distance which the fear of lupus has created between her and life. Nothing agreeable to her can be used as a means to attain her end. She must make use of something disgusting in order to create a justifiable distance between herself and life.

She acts correctly according to her system. If she did not have the accompanying feeling of hatred and loathing her behavior could rightly be called idiotic. There lies the difference between insanity and neurosis. A neurosis is always consistent, constructed on a scheme of private logic. Feeble-mindedness is inconsistent; it has no logical coherence or sequence whatsoever.

Father's objection that all other people existed without such fear was of no avail. It seemed to me as if lupus was there for me alone.

There you see how well she says it and still does not understand. The disease really exists for her.

A punishment for me alone.

This punishment must not be taken seriously. Nervous people say; "This is the punishment for my sins." This girl does not care about constructing a guilt complex if she can only exclude love.

THE CASE OF MISS R.

Like a horrible, gigantic spider the dread of the devouring disease crawled through me. If I had known of some way by which I could have killed myself quickly I would have done it. But I knew none.

She has not gotten far enough to cut off her life completely. She still has one resource, her family. Such a girl could be driven to suicide by separating her completely from her family: for instance, in a sanatorium where she was not well treated, or if her parents were to withdraw from her and declare her hopelessly insane. "Better dead than so to live." It might then happen that this girl would commit suicide as an act of revenge.

Miserable to the point of being almost feelingless, I commenced washing my hands and face with potassium permanganate. I rinsed my mouth thoroughly with Lina's antiseptic. I would not wear my coat again. I imagined that I had infected it by wearing it when I passed the lupus hospital. I wore gloves when I took my shoes off and was careful never to let the shoelaces touch the soles of the shoes which part I regarded as particularly badly infected. My parents watched my activities with great apprehension. Then I asked father whether it was possible to be infected by the air which came out of the lupus hospital. He laughed at me and answered that it was

A LUPUS PHOBIA

quite impossible, for otherwise, all the people who lived there or passed by would become ill.

That gave me a little hope. But I clung to the belief that the soles of my shoes were infected by having stepped on the same pavement on which the man with lupus had walked, and consequently, that the floor of our apartment was also infected. . . .

People who feel forced to wash themselves constantly (washing compulsion) usually use the argument that everything around them is dirty or infected. Such an argument serves to shut out some side of life in which they anticipate a defeat and in which they consequently do not feel secure. We have heard that the delusion was strengthened when she went out with the boy who praised another girl.

. . . and that perhaps one of the inmates had spit out of the window and I might have trodden on the slime. My parents tried desperately to pry me loose from this idea but in vain.

Her position in the house has now been firmly established. She has become the central figure, much more than before in that she has succeeded in cutting off all connection with the outside world.

From that time on I touched my shoes and coat only with gloves. One day a piece of lace slipped out of my hand to the floor. Mother had to give it away.

THE CASE OF MISS R.

I did not want to touch even mother any more since she had to come in contact with the floor when she washed and cleaned. My terrible excitement found vent in frequent crying spells. To quiet me my parents and Lina would touch the floor and my shoes with their fingers before my eyes. But later when mother cut the bread without first having washed her hands I shrieked and refused to eat. She had to get a new loaf. Even the doorknobs I touched only with gloves and, in addition, would cover the gloves with a piece of paper.

This is the usual trick of patients with a washing compulsion. As a consequence what follows is such filth in the room as one can expect only from people who ceaselessly wash themselves and, at the same time, continuously fight against dirt.

They had been infected by the infected hands of my family! Then I got the idea that one could never know whether money had been touched by a lupus sufferer or not. So I did not touch it any more unless I first covered my hand with a piece of paper. When I had to buy something, I wrapped the money in the inevitable paper and carried it to Minna. She had to accompany me and pay the bills.

Now she has a court marshal. Somebody has to accompany her on the street. That is an agoraphobia.*

---

* Fear of being left alone or going out alone.

A LUPUS PHOBIA

She also had to open doors for me because door-knobs were suspicious. A beggar suffering from lupus might have touched them! Dirt, misery, poverty seemed to me grounds for lupus.

In this respect she is not quite wrong.

Finally I did not touch anything any more without paper. When I wanted to move a chair from one spot to another, or when I had to pass an object, for instance, a brush, to some one, I first protected myself with paper. A pair of gloves with which I had taken up some money I threw away because I had forgotten the paper. I wrapped pencils in paper before writing with them. My frightened thoughts were running in so many different directions that at last there was nothing left that I did not believe to be infected.

I remember a wild discussion between a patient with a washing compulsion neurosis and a chemist in which the patient wanted to prove that no place in the world was absolutely free from particles of dirt.

The chemist denied it. I was on the patient's side; it seemed to me that she was right. But whether she was right or not was of no consequence. What matters is to make progress in life, to make oneself useful. One does not make oneself useful by declaring that everything is dirty and then resting on one's oars.

THE CASE OF MISS R.

One day I took a walk with a school friend and her mother. Suddenly I saw a terrible looking man with a red, swollen face full of holes. He was standing near the curb. I asked my friend to look at him. She did and burst out laughing. I myself was not able to look again in his direction. I was glad we were walking on the other side of the pavement. I thought this girl would, of a surety, become infected with lupus as punishment for ridiculing him.

Again I must insert a few remarks. People suffering from phobias and other forms of neurosis frequently imagine that they are pursued by diabolic, relentless misfortune. I do not believe that many among you have met a lupus sufferer more than once. This girl has met such a diseased person at least twice. One often hears that neurotics constantly have an experience repeated. I remember a case of washing compulsion—a woman who examined everything in the world for dirt in order to eliminate dirt. I have never seen any one who was so much in contact with dirt as she was. I shall try to explain this in a few words.

We have seen that a neurotic is always seeking justifications to protect and strengthen his asocial attitude. His feelings have led him into a neurosis; his understanding which is not distorted, has not followed his feelings, cannot follow, and is forced continually to produce means to lessen the tension

A LUPUS PHOBIA

between intellect and feeling. Reason is taken in tow by feeling and reason thereupon holds it its task to demonstrate that such a restricted field of activity is inevitable. And so we see the patient pursuing vindicating arguments or facts, and especially such facts as appear to him fatefully inevitable, like acts of God for which he is not responsible.

We must remember the extraordinary ability of the psyche to arrange, correct, choose, exclude and purposively apperceive. When we remember this, we can then understand that where the psychical apparatus has become the instrument of a neurotic goal, the intellect, governed by feelings, arranges, chooses and purposively apperceives such facts as will not disturb the neurotic development, or the neurotic goal, and the neurotic finally appears to us as a poor, pitiable victim of circumstance. He plays a trick and is fooled by it himself.

For example, a man says he wants to get married and have a child. He falls in love with one girl after another and each one rejects him. The result is that he is in exactly the same spot after twenty years as he was when he started; namely, unmarried. The world pities him since he obviously makes every effort to win a wife. The world does not bother to examine the sincerity of his efforts very closely. If it did, it would see that he probably always approaches a type which he knows in advance will

THE CASE OF MISS R.

refuse him; or that he makes his courtship so clumsy an affair that he is sure to be unsuccessful; or that his behavior toward the woman makes him impossible as a prospective husband; in short, that he does everything to prevent the actual steps leading to a marriage in order that he may remain within the fortress he has built because of his fear of women.

This is an example of the art and cunning of neurotic thought and argument, somewhat simplified and schematized, naturally, in order to make it more understandable. But the example achieves its purpose when it clarifies the fact that not the experiences which one has are important, but the lessons one learns from these experiences, and that correct interpretation of experience is necessary to understand another human being. With this peculiarity of the human intellect in mind, one no longer questions whether those disturbances and misfortunes in neurotic life which are frequently repeated are merely accidents or whether there exists a tendency among neurotics to run after their blows.

I brought Minna two pieces of sugar which I had first rubbed on the soles of my shoes.

You see how far the tendency to degrade goes. She attacks all other persons as if she had to exterminate them because she feels unable to cope with them. She only is worth while, and she only is to be respected.

A LUPUS PHOBIA

I was frantic with joy when she ate them.

This is an excessive form of egotism which is converted into criminal trends. There is no doubt that her egotism expresses itself in the tendency to degrade. She approaches her fellow human beings in an aggressive manner; that is egotism. One may call it by another name, but every one will have to agree that she is an individual who is interested in her own person exclusively. The Freudian school calls this manifestation narcissism. The word "narcissism" is taken from the story of the Greek youth who fell in love with his mirrored reflection. Narcissism plays an important rôle in Freudian psychology. It is the libidinous love of a person for himself. Every person is supposed to have a greater or smaller narcissistic love for himself. To those acquainted with psychological literature I suggest the consideration that narcissism certainly does not include the conception of egotism and the tendency to degrade.

I really thought she would get a little lupus from eating the sugar. I then fed all my friends with that sort of sugar but gave none to my family. When I had to go through the street where the lupus man passed, I held my clothes close to my body in the fear that the lupus man might have touched the walls of the houses and the lamp-posts. But I often imagined that a part of the dress had somehow grazed

THE CASE OF MISS R.

one of those spots. Then I ran straight home and hurriedly took off all my clothes. But when I passed this street with a friend, I would push her, seemingly by accident, against the walls and lamp-posts so that she should get some bacilli on her dress too.

At this point we must remember that the outbreak of lupus phobia occurred when she took a walk with a boy who liked another girl as well. Her gesture expresses clearly that she wants to exclude this other girl—every girl.

And when I thought that a piece of clothing had become infected, I threw it away. But since my wardrobe was in a sad condition, I wondered how I could help myself. I conceived the idea of letting father destroy the bacteria with his hot iron and moist cloth.

She has discovered a working method which was later on proven correct by scientific research.

My family frequently had to go through the dangerous street. I asked them repeatedly to be careful not to touch anything there. Although they promised it over and over again the suspicion would not leave me that they did not pay any attention to my caution. Now none of them was allowed to come near me any more.

You see how she aggravates her condition. Her radius of activity becomes smaller and smaller. She

A LUPUS PHOBIA

is the only one in the world who is pure, free from bacilli, the only one who realizes how all others plunge into misery. All other people are profane, depraved, infected; only she is not. She is a saint. It is the goal of superiority on the useless side of life which she achieves by cheap means.

And when some one touched me by accident I raved and stormed, had crying spells and threatened to kill myself. I did not know any more where to sit down so as to be far enough from the others. I used only one and the same chair and no one else was allowed to sit on it.

Does this not remind you of certain customs of monarchs or religious customs where a certain seat may be touched only by a sacred person? If some one were to assert now that the girl derives these ideas from archaic, inherited traditions, we have only one answer: everybody gets the same silly ideas under similar, restrictive conditions.

I also selected my own knives, forks and spoons which were put in a certain place to be protected from infection by the rest of the furniture. I took strict care of my things. Woe if mother happened to put a wrong fork on my special plate!

You see what you can observe in every neurotic; she is sick. That means a law for the others. The

THE CASE OF MISS R.

others receive regulations for their lives from the disease of the neurotic. That gives her a feeling of superiority even if she does not notice it. I do not believe that this fact can be overlooked by anybody whose attention has ever been called to it.

One day, during house cleaning, my water glass with my toothbrush in it was accidentally put on the table. When I saw that I grew furious, swore at my mother in vile language, menaced her, threatened to kill her—I don't know what else I did in my rage.

It almost looks like the divine wrath of a god when some one has violated his sacred commands.

Such scenes occurred practically every day. Then my parents would wrangle about me. Father would accuse mother of not having been careful enough and thus having excited me. Mother would reply angrily that she could not keep all my caprices in mind, that she had other things to think of. Our employes also trembled in my presence.

I do not know whether that is quite true, but it is sufficient that she has the impression.

When I was on the street I was always anticipating meeting perforated faces. The whole city was soon inhabited by lupus sufferers. I saw them everywhere. I did not dare go out any more at night for fear I might bump into one of them in the dark.

212

A LUPUS PHOBIA

The restriction goes farther.

In the daytime I stared at all faces, and when some one passed by too quickly for me to see whether he had a nose or not, I ran after him and stared at him again. Every time I imagined, "This one has had lupus." Then I would rush home crying and complain to father, "I have seen a lupus sufferer again." Father always tried to talk me out of my delusion. His clear and sensible explanations quieted me every time to a certain degree. He was the only one able to console me a little from time to time.

This "from time to time" needs some further consideration. It means almost nothing. She may permit herself to be consoled by her father—in order to be able to start again. Physicians often hear their patients say, "When I leave your office I feel fine. But as soon as I am out it starts all over again." Many doctors believe it is a magic power emanating from them. However, what it amounts to is that a patient makes the physician the present of a compliment in order to lead him astray. We usually answer, "Then you should stay here all day." The fascination then vanishes quickly.

I washed myself constantly with potassium permanganate. The skin of my hands became terribly rough, as hard as leather and full of cracks.

THE CASE OF MISS R.

That is correct. One will remark that people who feel compelled to wash themselves all day have the dirtiest hands in the world.

My teeth became brown from continual rinsing. When the soap or a brush fell on the floor I did not use it again. Not for a kingdom would I have picked up something from the floor. Mother also had to wash her hands ceaselessly. I watched her narrowly, especially before she started to cook. If she forgot to wash her hands I did not eat one morsel, however hungry I may have been. The restrictions I imposed on her irritated her and she complained to father. He begged her to indulge me.

You will observe how her power extends farther and farther. He who does not comprehend this does not comprehend the most important facts. Unlimited power is most important to her, and though there is only a small circle at her disposal she does as much as possible to dominate it.

I had the most inconvenient difficulties with my shoelaces. If one of them touched the soles of my shoes or the floor mother had to pull it out immediately and buy a new one. I had assembled a whole collection of infected shoelaces in a drawer. I also had a full line of hair pins, soaps, toothbrushes and dental creams. Father was already considering consulting

A LUPUS PHOBIA

a physician. My delusion was kept secret from ousiders.

As a rule parents keep the ailment secret in a kind of false shame without helping the child by doing so. On the other hand, if they speak too much about it it is of no advantage, either. One should find a method which helps everybody.

When I found an illustration of the so-called lupus spoon in Lina's instrument book I shuddered. I wondered why there was only one instrument for such an abominable disease.

She regards it as an insult, a degradation of her bugbear, that there is but one instrument for it.

Lina told me that one could get lupus not only on the face but all over the body as well. I did not dread that so much as the image of a face full of holes.

He who observes a little more closely knows why. "She is the fairest in the land." Therefore the stress laid on the facial lupus.

I brooded ceaselessly on the lupus disease. Horrible things came to my mind. I imagined, for instance, that a lupus sufferer touches one with his fingers after having touched his wounds or scratched them. Or that a drop of pus comes in contact with a coin which one unsuspectingly takes in one's hand

THE CASE OF MISS R.

—then one may scratch one's own eye which would, no doubt, infect a person with lupus.

She understands something about inoculation; that is, infecting an eye by bringing a germ in direct contact with it.

The thought especially that a lupus sufferer might kiss me made me shiver with fright.

This *"especially"* is charming.

Finally I fancied that the mere thought of contact with lupus might produce the disease, that the thought might be as much as the act.

Here again she anticipates some of the modern theories and hypotheses. Right now the conception of "mind over matter" is widely spread.

When such thoughts came to my mind I became extremely excited, washed my face in a hurry and ran to father to get some consolation. However, I had to overcome some reluctance to speak of these ideas, tried first to indicate, to circumscribe them, never said directly: "I have imagined this or that," but: "If a girl were to imagine this, and so on."

Her conscience is not clear. She does not want to assume any responsibility for her neurosis. She has some glimmering that her attitude is unjustifiable and

A LUPUS PHOBIA

will not admit it. As long as she does not understand and interpret correctly her intentions and striving, she finds no way out and goes on further, like a Don Quixote, to fight windmills.

I also often thought—we lived on the ground floor—how easily some one could climb in the window—and, what is more, it might be a lupus sufferer!

Two evils at once.

"Such sufferers," I said to myself, "must always be in great need, because they are avoided by other people."

Here again let us find out what there is behind those words. One could say, for instance: as a result they have to be helped. He who speaks thus is on the useful side. She continues differently. One has to beware of such cunning rascals. You see when two persons have the same impression, the same experience, they draw different conclusions according to their different goals and different style of life.

The idea of a burglar with lupus scared me to death. Then I remembered a story which I had read or heard somewhere in which God tries a saint with a leper—I thought that was the same as lupus. The leper very soon turned out to be the Lord Himself. And I said to myself: "Even were the Lord Himself to come as a lupus sufferer to me I should not admit

217

THE CASE OF MISS R.

Him; indeed I should not touch Him—or should I make an exception in that case?"

One day we went on an excursion. I was in the third grade in school, I believe. Coming back we passed a new lupus hospital; in fact, I don't know whether there were or are two lupus hospitals in this city. I'll find out. Suddenly I read in big letters, "Hospital for Lupus Sufferers." That gave me a sad feeling. I must have known at that time what lupus is. There was a milkstand on the station where we had to transfer to another car. Our boarder was with us. Father bought hot milk for us. I also drank a glass. But with the lupus hospital before my eyes I detested the milk. I had a dim feeling that a lupus sufferer had drunk out of my glass.

That is an old remembrance. What conclusion can we draw from it? No more and no less than that she is now endeavoring to support her lupus phobia. She searches until she finds new justifications for the continuation of her neurosis. You will frequently find in the psychology of neurotics that they search for support for the present scheme in their past life.

In the meantime our circumstances had changed for the worse. Many of father's customers had been drafted for military service, some of them without having paid their bills. We could hardly pay the relatively high rent of our apartment. At the first

A LUPUS PHOBIA

opportunity we moved into a house some blocks further on. It was an old house and our new home was cheaper and roomier than the old one and was on the first floor. Up to that time I had slept between my parents. Now I got a little room to share with Lina and, for the first time, a bed of my own. Lina slept on the couch.

We already understand enough of the character of this girl to be able to guess what is going to follow. She will probably not want to lie there all alone. She will not let herself be driven out of an agreeable situation. She has mentioned this fact before. It is supposed to express: "I am the center." That means a description in space for her psychic construction.

I did not want to be driven so abruptly out of the bed of my parents in which I had slept so long. For some time I remained—as a temporary arrangement —in mother's bed. Gradually I decided to reconcile myself to the new custom. Little by little the lupus delusion, which had harassed me for over a year, disappeared.

What that has to do with sleeping alone is not quite intelligible. However, there might be a relation between the two facts. We have assumed that the lupus phobia is directed against every possible relation with men, that she is afraid of the love problem. She sleeps alone; she emphasizes that the lupus phobia is

THE CASE OF MISS R.

disappearing. Perhaps she is relieved by the thought: "One can remain single." I do not know whether we shall find my assumption confirmed. I shall follow this idea very carefully, awaiting further corroboration.

I could not put up with lying alone at night very long. Besides, my bed was unsteady and I was afraid that the upper part might fall down on me and smash my teeth or crush my nose.

Again a beauty defect.

I was quite particular about my nose. When Lina gave me a kiss I often imagined she had distorted it. Then the tapping of a woodworm made me nervous. Every other day my sister had night duty, and I felt all the more lonely.

The sister suits her purpose very well. We see how the tendency to withdraw from men leads her to her sister. Before she slept alone she chose to lie beside her mother. We shall have to see whether she is struggling to save herself from the confused state of her erotic problems, whether or not her refusal of men and attachment to women are growing stronger.

I asked mother, to sleep in my bed while I slept in hers.

This would disprove our combination if we should, as other psychological schools, recognize the man in

A LUPUS PHOBIA

her father. According to their interpretation the desire to sleep in her mother's bed would indicate a wish to approach her father sexually and eliminate her mother of whom she is jealous. However, her father is unquestionably asexual for her; we do not know yet why she goes through this performance.

At that time I had the custom of hanging my stockings and garters over father's bedstead before going to sleep; on top I put my hairpins; I spread my shirt, petticoat and bloomers on his comforter, and my shoes I put under his bed. I laid my dress, sweater, coat and hat carefully on the table. No one was permitted to touch these things lest I become wild with fury. One night, lying awake, I noticed that father continually slapped his face in his sleep. The action frightened me—I thought he was going crazy. Suddenly he opened his eyes and exclaimed: "What is tickling my nose?" And then I saw that my garters were doing it. The fear that the head piece of the bed might fall on me did not let me sleep peacefully in mother's bed, so I had to take it down every evening before getting into bed. Soon a new cause for alarm appeared. Over the little night table, standing between father's and mother's beds . . .

The beds are separated. She plays the rôle of the mother since she is using her mother's bed, but sleeping separated from her father.

THE CASE OF MISS R.

. . . hung an image of the Holy Virgin. The image was a little nearer my side. I became anxious about that. I imagined it might fall down on me. On the other hand I was too superstitious to have it removed. So I went back to my own bedroom and bed.

When we consider the situation of this girl, we realize that pampered children leave places to which they have been long accustomed very reluctantly.

In the middle of one night I fell through my bed with a crash. That made the bed all the more unattractive to me and I slept thereafter in mother's bed with her. In order to be safe from the holy image I moved over to the very edge of the bed. I cannot say that this position was very comfortable. Besides, I still did not feel safe enough. I often got up when all the others were asleep, stood for a while somewhere in the room in my nightgown and pondered on how I could get rid of the bed troubles. One night, while I was standing in my former bedroom and brooding, I accidentally made some noise. Lina awoke, jumped up terror-stricken and began to cry pitifully. She believed she was face to face with a ghost. I crept quickly back to bed. The menacing image on the wall drove my sleep away. I then tried to lie in bed the other way round, my head near mother's feet. But that was more uncomfortable than before. Our feet hit each other's face during the night. Finally father

A LUPUS PHOBIA

took my vacant bed and let me sleep in his bed. Even there I did not feel quite at ease. I do not know why I believed this bed would bring me bad luck.

That seems to agree with the idea that it is dangerous to get too near a man.

Then it was arranged in the following way: father returned to his bed, Lina took my bed and I slept on Lina's couch. But the couch was too short for me. I was considerably taller than my sister and had long legs. My feet hung over the end of the couch. I had to wrap them in a special blanket. Then mother had the idea of preparing my bed in the kitchen on the sewing table. But the table was too hard and a draft from a nearby window disturbed me.

This child certainly has many difficulties in bed.

Now we resolved that I should try to sleep with father in his bed. But since, in fear of the holy image, I lay down in the direction reverse to the one in which he lay, the arrangement was as awkward as it had been in mother's bed. At last, father ordered a carpenter to repair my bed while I watched him do it. Then I lay down, head at the wrong end, and so it remained.

The position which a person assumes in sleep is certainly not accidental and seems to have some significance in judging his style of life. Individual psy-

THE CASE OF MISS R.

chological investigation has shown us that even the phenomenon of sleep is patterned on the person's style of life. Those who understand individual psychology can often guess the position assumed in sleep by others.

Experience has taught us, for instance, that people who sleep on their stomachs are usually stubborn. We can hardly expect a person to exhibit much courage in life who goes to sleep by rolling himself up like a porcupine and pulling the blankets over his head. A young man sleeps with his arms crossed on his chest. His style of life reveals a desire to imitate Napoleon. Later, when life is hard, he conceives the insane idea that he has been chosen general to lead troops into Russia. Our girl lies in bed wrong end to. Her position expresses opposition—nothing else, although, of course, such persons may also assume an oppositional attitude in regard to their love relations.

After finishing high school father wanted me to take up dressmaking.

We hardly believe she will take up dressmaking because that is a subordinate profession.

But I did not care for it. I would rather have ntered business school like Olga who set the example jor me in every way. Father did not consent. He ..ggested that it would cost too much. He preferred to have me become a pianist and spoke of a

224

A LUPUS PHOBIA

scholarship in a conservatory. I replied; "And then? Then I shall be a stupid piano teacher!" Finally we came to no decision whatsoever and I remained at home.

That is the right place.

Next fall I registered for a one year course at business school. I was the only one in the class who paid her tuition fee monthly. All but two or three of my classmates came from wealthy families. I felt happy in their company. I made friends with the prettiest and most distinguished ones and was invited to their homes. But since I could never invite them to our house—I had told them a lot of lies about our circumstances—our friendships did not become as intimate as my friendship with Olga. I could speak of things with her which would have shocked the wealthier girls. Although I hated moral conversations I always made myself listen patiently. My greatest wish was to prolong these acquaintance-ships. . . . I remember a very disagreeable episode. We could buy liberty bonds at school. This was done in the following way: the professor called out our names in alphabetical order and asked every one of us, naming in addition our father's profession, how many bonds we wanted to buy. Almost all the girls had permission from their parents to buy bonds and named smaller or larger amounts. Meanwhile I was

THE CASE OF MISS R.

on pins and needles. Not only that father could not spare one cent more for war contributions—we were glad when we could get an extra loaf of bread from time to time—but it was going to be revealed in public that father was a tailor. Slowly my doom approached. When my name was called out, I arose, blushing all over. The professor cast a glance at the list and said: "Your father is a tailor. Tailors make much money nowadays." I do not remember what I stammered in answer . . . I was a pretty good scholar in general, but arithmetic and bookkeeping were my weak points. The morning before an examination in arithmetic, I would say to my father; "I feel so ill, I can hardly stand up straight . . ."

That is common. If a child trains for it properly it becomes automatic, so that she feels sick upon merely hearing the word arithmetic. *"It makes me sick to hear of it."* One also notices this mechanism in other situations where it is harder to explain. Headaches, tiredness, even vomiting, often originate this way. A teacher, for instance, had a fright spell when he approached the city hall in his town. Without knowing anything about him, it would be impossible to understand what the city hall has to do with the spell. The reason in this case was that he had to report to the higher school officials. Another time, at a party, he was asked when he had to go to school. Five minutes later he had another fear spell. This be-

226

A LUPUS PHOBIA

comes intelligible only upon due consideration of the facts that have led to this condition.

". . . and went back to bed. The following day I went to school again. Eventually the professor of arithmetic discovered my trick and gave me the lowest mark every time I did not attend school. One day I was impertinent to a professor and got a low mark in conduct. On such occasions we had to take a report home and return it with one parent's signature. Although I had no reason to be afraid of father I decided to get his signature on that piece of paper without letting him know what he was signing. To that end I proceeded as follows: I took a sheet of white paper, covered it with a small strip of red blotting paper, leaving only a small margin, went to father and begged him to write his name in the white margin. First, of course, he wanted to see what was under the blotting paper. I took it away and there was nothing but a blank sheet of white paper. He asked, astonished, what I wanted it for. I only smiled. He probably thought this was another one of my whims, wrote his name and shook his head.

The fight with her teacher is almost a pleasure to her; she tries to get the upper hand over him and succeeds. She won a lasting victory over her father long ago.

'After a while I did the same thing again, and once

227

THE CASE OF MISS R.

more father wanted to see the covered paper first. The third time, however, he signed without looking. This time he had signed the conduct report. . . . Our classes were between two and six o'clock. In the forenoon I studied—as a matter of fact only before an examination. Mother then heated the little stove in the bedroom. Father worked in the kitchen with his assistants late into the night. The customers came and went during the day. We were never by ourselves, never undisturbed. The assistants had to work on Sunday morning and in the afternoon customers tried on their suits. Mother, Lina and I hated this state of affairs. We tried to persuade father to work at certain hours, like other tailors, and then rest. But we could not convince him. He always answered: "You hate the tailoring business. But without my work you wouldn't have anything to eat." We had just enough to eat, but otherwise, in spite of all the work, we were in need of almost everything. Father had gradually acquired the fixed idea of working for an unusually low price, for almost cost price. Sewing was his passion, to produce good suits his pleasure, to satisfy his customers his ambition and pride. Even when he had so many orders that the assistants had to work overtime, there was often hardly enough money left at the end of the week to pay them their wages. Lina always had to help, although

228

A LUPUS PHOBIA

all she had was her meagre salary. A relative wanted to keep the books for father or even help him to open a store where he would have had nothing to do but cut and fit. But father's initiative had been killed; one could not get him away from sewing.

That illustrates well the inflexible automatism of older age. A life's training cannot be easily broken and should be broken only when it is necessary for the individual and his environment. I must confess I should not try either to detach such an automatized worker from his work. I should not say to an elderly man that he ought to stop working, or entirely rearrange his scheme of work, because he would feel life pressing upon him heavily as soon as the automatization ceased.

Father's craze to make a present of his labor to his customers brought about terrible family quarrels. Mother, with Lina's backing, showered father with reproaches, scolded him, yelled that this life was no life and that he was ruining all of us, asked him what he thought would become of the child. At first he would answer, but as soon as mother mentioned my name he became silent, went into the bedroom and tore his hair.

One day, brushing crumbs off the table, I carelessly dropped my pocket mirror on the floor. Upon

THE CASE OF MISS R.

picking it up, I saw that it had a few cracks. "How silly," I thought, "now I shan't have good luck for seven years."

Here is another opportunity for compulsion thoughts and compulsion acts. This is the third time—a proof that the disappearance of one symptom (the lupus phobia, for example) is no indication of a cure, but that a new symptom will be produced, and that the appearance of symptoms will not stop as long as she does not change her goal and style of life. Besides, I want to emphasize the fact that neurotics are always superstitious. It is comprehensible that every one who does not believe in himself has to believe in something else, whatever it may be. It does not, of course, follow that because you believe in something else you do not believe in yourself.

On that day I was somewhat depressed. I went to Olga to ask her whether she had ever broken a mirror. She could not remember ever having done so. I thereupon decided to have her break a mirror at an opportune moment so that she would have no good luck for seven years either.

You see how she constantly strives for equality in so far as others are not to be better off than she.

A little later Lina was angry for some reason or other and broke her mirror in a fit of wrath. I ap-

A LUPUS PHOBIA

proached the fragments gingerly, looked at them and wondered how my sister could break a mirror, knowing the while that she would not have good luck for seven years. . . . In the coatroom of the business school, one of the girls accidentally dropped her pocket mirror while taking off her coat. I was standing behind her at the moment and she cried jokingly: "Oh, goodness, now you have broken my mirror!" I was startled. She quieted me, assuring me that she herself had broken it, not I. I was badly frightened and asked her if she were quite sure of it. She swore that it was so. I believed her since I had hardly touched the mirror, and when I looked at her, I thought: "Whether or not she has broken a mirror makes no difference. She is not pretty and will have no good luck anyway."

There you have further evidence for the correctness of our assumption that her main object is to be pretty enough to be the first one in life.

I remember, by the way . . .

She is collecting memories again to support her neurotic behavior.

. . . that as a small child I was once afraid of a mirror. I was passing a glassware store and looked into one of the mirrors on display. From it a horribly swollen face stared back at me.

231

THE CASE OF MISS R.

Again the swollen face!

I recoiled, but could not resist looking back a second time. Alongside this mirror hung another that distorted my face lengthwise in a weird fashion. Father explained to me afterwards that these were mirrors which distorted all they reflected. Our petroleum lamp had a reflector to make the light shine more brightly. This mirror, or reflector, had already bothered me, as I remember now, at the time of my eye phobia. It now began to disturb me very much. I would not touch the lamp. I was often asked to carry it from the kitchen to the living room when father had a customer, but even if fifty customers had waited outside, I could no longer be made to touch that lamp. I was afraid the mirror might break on account of the intense heat of the petroleum flame and the resulting bad luck would attach itself to me if I just happened to be present. I let the others sit by the lamp and took my seat further away. Realizing, however, that it was all the same whether my parents or Lina or I were near the mirror when it broke, since the mischief would then pursue us all, I begged father to take the reflector off the lamp. This done, I worried about what they would do with it. Mother wanted to throw it in the garbage can. I objected because it might break in there. Then she proposed giving it away. I did not like that either. I thought that

A LUPUS PHOBIA

might also mean bad luck. Finally we stored it in a wooden box in the cellar.

You see to what lengths she goes in an effort to avoid all possible bad luck. And you also see with what super-caution, wrongly placed of course, she nourishes the idea that one can somehow force one's fate. This wretched phobia contains the idea of godliness. What must I do in order to control fate?

CHAPTER XI

YES! BUT—

*F*ATHER *had a little work basket of plaited straw in which he kept, among other things, several pocket mirrors. I was afraid to break them, and was always very careful not to touch the basket. Finally father decided to sell the mirrors to the same man who bought our remnants.*

Her attention is concentrated more and more upon all mirrors around her. Such a preoccupation is important and significant for the structure of every neurosis, becoming most conspicuous in a compulsion neurosis. What really happens is quite intelligible to the individual psychologist. All the other social tasks of life are placed in the background. The patient has abandoned her duties. She stands a greater distance away from the important problems of her life. She spends all her time occupying herself uselessly in order not to suffer a defeat in trying to solve her problems on the generally useful side of life.

We know that this extremely spoiled child is striving for a goal of superiority, that she wants to be

YES! BUT—

more than all the others. We have seen how she succeeded in attaining her goal within her family. Now, as she grows older, she has to approach the community outside her family. That is the present situation. Her success is thoroughly uncertain. Like all pampered children she abjures, on general principles, all new situations, all the more so, the less certain she is of her success. Her striving to remain within the old situation and attempt to achieve there the goal of superiority thereby becomes more apparent. This is easily accomplished by means of a neurosis whose intensity can be increased in accordance with the purpose. The father especially, and the other members of the family as well, are drawn into the whirl of her fixed ideas which gives her the impression of her superiority in the house.

The symptomatic choice of the mirror now becomes obvious. As in former years, the girl makes her principal object in life being first or foremost although she now moves in a broader circle and nearer the front of life. Problems of love and marriage come closer. *Shall I be able to surpass other girls in my relations with men; shall I gain power over men?* Her interest concentrates itself distinctly around the mirror, probably stimulated by her visual training. Occasionally she complains of her weak eyes. It is natural that children with more or less minor eye defects increase their interest in all

THE CASE OF MISS R.

visible objects in order to conquer their difficulties. In this way they become more closely acquainted with colors, lines, shades, perspective and usually retain this visual interest for the rest of their lives.

However, this girl has become uncertain, vacillating, as almost all pampered children do when they have to face a new situation. Her tendency is to solve the problems of love and of sex in the same fashion as she has tried to solve all problems up to now; that is to say, she wants to be the foremost. Love and marriage, however, are social problems. Their solution requires interest in others. Her prototype lacks such interest in others almost entirely, which is typical for pampered children. She wants to master the others, force them to obey her command. Will she be able to do the same in love? The marriage of her parents, her whole environment perhaps, does not give her the impression of the unimpeded victoriousness of woman. Love becomes a dangerous obstacle to her desire to rule; she is not at all certain of conquering it in her favor. The thus intensified feeling of uncertainty causes her to shake off responsibility from her person and shift it onto mirrors. Her fate depends on mirrors now. But suppose the mirror breaks?

A widely spread superstition makes a happy marriage depend upon whether one has broken a mirror. A strange, spiteful magic has to decide. Not the

YES! BUT—

magic effect of one's own personality. If she is not the first in the contest of love, then it is the mirror's fault, and her superiority is not touched. She who breaks a mirror cannot marry for seven years; so runs the superstition. That would exempt her from having to decide whether she is the "first in the country." But she could continue to believe so. Like all pampered children she is hunting for easier means whereby to gain the final victory.

Two general remarks may be inserted here. A few of my critics, unfortunately blinded by rage, believe that I have eradicated sexuality and love from my psychological conception. I wish to point out, however, that here, as in all cases of neuroses and psychoses, as well as in perversions, one does not meet with love in the light of common sense, that is, as an attribute of the social feeling, but only sexual desire in the service of a striving for power on the generally useless side of life. Both sexual desire and striving for power have switched over from the tracks of general usefulness onto the tracks of neurosis and both no longer share in the progress of humanity, but are part of personal egotism.

Secondly, I want to emphasize the fact that this unwise employment of our love potentialities encounters difficulties everywhere. As love and marriage are tasks for two persons, there is no room for egocentric presumptions on the part of one of them.

THE CASE OF MISS R.

Moreover, the partner's response to the unsatisfactory advances of the neurotic is naturally unfavorable. And above all, the neurotic always feels hurt when his timid social feeling is challenged as it is by all problems of life, since all problems of life (birth of children, school, friendship, interest in mankind, political standpoint, profession, love, marriage) are social problems. Regarding the love problems of the neurotic one will always be able to perceive a diminishing speed in his activities to the point of a hesitating attitude or complete standstill. The violent aggression in the beginning is followed by a sudden end. From a physical point of view this description is sufficiently clear. Physical expression of the disturbance is found in impotence, vaginism, frigidity, perversions, ejaculatio precox, etc. This superstitious occupation with mirrors exhibits the hesitating attitude of the girl. If a mirror breaks, this accident is blamed in case she does not win, and her superiority saved. Every now and then the thought of committing suicide appears. Death seems salvation, the last consolation of the desperate.

The objection might be raised: why is she anxious about breaking a mirror since the resulting bad luck would help her to avoid the problem of love, and protected by her superstition, she would not even have to make an attempt to occupy herself with the dangerous question. The neurotic does not think so

YES! BUT—

simply. She wants to have an appearance of making every effort to respond to the demands of communal life. That is her "yes." But then she throws a stone in her way which impedes her progress. That is her "but." And the result is that she has a good alibi for the evasion of the danger of love; she has reneged. I want to very much BUT I cannot. That is the meaning of her fear of mirrors. As long as some one wants to, but excuses himself with a "but," he does *not* want to.

Several mirrors were displayed in the shop window of the candy store that Tilda's mother owned. Up till then I had not noticed them. One day I suddenly imagined I had smashed one of the mirrors by closing the store door, and I was seized with a terrible fright. Tilda examined all the mirrors in the window carefully and swore that she could not detect a crack in any one of them. But I did not believe her and was so unhappy all day long that I wanted to die. I said to myself: "I'll have misfortune for seven years anyway—and now seven more years in addition; then I'll have no more happiness at all in life and it would be better to die now."

The next day I was quiet again; but from then on when I went to see Tilda I took Minna with me to open and close the door.

Every time I accidentally touched a woman with a pocketbook, on the street or in the street car, the

239

THE CASE OF MISS R.

fearful thought struck me like lightning that I had demolished her pocket-mirror and thus caused myself seven more years of misfortune. Frequently I followed such a woman and wanted to ask her whether she really carried a mirror in her pocketbook and, if so, whether it was still intact. But I never dared do so.

As long as the question is not answered the possibility remains that a mirror has been broken. Therefore she does not dare to ask.

I had to use a mirror when I wanted to comb my hair. I possessed a square hand mirror which I touched only with the greatest precaution. Sometimes I fancied that I had put it too roughly on the table, and, at the same time, thought I had heard it crack. Then I ran to my parents or Lina full of fear—they had to inspect it thoroughly. And even if they swore by all they held holy that they could not see any crack, not even a scratch, I did not believe them and I trusted my own eyes still less. I was bent madly on the thought that there was a crack in it, perhaps not perceptible to the naked eye.

In order to see whether it would break I now put the mirror on the table as carefully as possible. And immediately I fancied again that I had broken it. The longer I manipulated it in this manner the more strongly I labored under this delusion and the

240

YES! BUT—

more excited I became. After a while I was raving.

One day on the street we passed the fragments of a mirror. The idea that I had touched them with my foot grew in an instant to the conviction that I had stepped on them. I ran home weeping and complained to father: "Something terrible has happened to me."

In an alarmed tone he asked what it was. At first I did not want to tell. Merely to speak about it seemed calamitous to me. I felt as miserable as if I had just been sentenced to death. At his insistent request I told him what had happened.

The mirror story cannot be exaggerated enough. A frequent occurrence in a neurosis to achieve the purpose at any cost.

Father laughed and said that according to my own description some one else and not I had broken the mirror. I had only come in contact with the fragments which certainly did not forbode anything. But this time he could not console me. Then I called Minna and led her to the spot where the fragments were lying, without letting her know at what I was aiming. I took her arm and ingeniously arranged to have her step unsuspectingly on the glass. Now I felt easier. I thought, "If I have no more luck you shall not have any more luck either!"

Struggling against the superiority of others. As if it were proof that this actually has to do with her

241

THE CASE OF MISS R.

love problem, the son of the proprietor of the café appears on the scene at the right moment.

I was very friendly with the son of the proprietor of our favorite café. We had already played together when we were children. His name was Hans and he was just as old as I. He had a speech defect. His vocal cords had been hurt in a tonsil operation.

We often took walks together. But since I disliked being alone with a boy and wanted to make some new acquaintances I asked him one day whether he did not know of a friend for me.

Two are less than one. This is a frequent neurotic phenomenon in case there is some possibility of affection for a person, in order to prevent a love affair. One cannot be in love with two persons at the same time without lying to oneself. When one cannot decide for one or the other this indecision is the decision. Neither one is wanted. The phenomenon of indecision appears frequently in life and indicates always a tendency to refuse.

The attempts of the girl to approach love relations, although they are very careful, do not surprise us. They are attempts to say yes in situations of little danger, in much the same way as some one who seems about to decide to withdraw, yet makes a few hesitating steps forward only to express his but. This "yes!—but . . ." as we said before, is perhaps the

YES! BUT—

best definition of the neurosis. In the following paragraphs we shall have our opinion confirmed and see how she handles a love affair.

In return for it I was to introduce him to my friend Olga. Then the four of us could go out together. He replied that he knew many boys and that he would find a suitable one. I made it a condition that my boy friend had to be handsome.

Fritz, the friend, was a tall, blond fellow who, in spite of his youth, liked to show off as a man of the world. He was immediately attracted to me and told me a lot of nonsense. I also told him a pack of lies. . . .

When I asked Hans how he liked Olga, he said: "Quite well, only her manners are not so good yet"; and then, for his taste she was too dull . . . he liked a lively girl better. He was only fifteen years old and stole money from his father when he wanted to go to the movies with a girl. I replied: "What do you think? You must know how to take her. My dear, she has had a lot of experience—why don't you try it?"

And I summed up all her nice qualities. I myself did not want to be alone with Fritz. I always wanted the other two to be with us. Hans, who was easily influenced by me, promised to go with us the next time. In return I gave him my word to find another girl for him if he did not want Olga any more.

THE CASE OF MISS R.

Fritz was very much in love with me. In the movies he made bashful advances. But I rejected him with the words: "I prefer to talk at a certain distance." He had to follow suit.

One evening Hans rushed into the room in great excitement, saying that Fritz had taken a box at the People's Opera House for "Rigoletto" and that I should get dressed in a hurry. I did not quite like the idea. I was a little ashamed to appear with the two boys in a box. But since my parents did not object I got ready quickly. Fritz was already awaiting us in the box. He handed me a bunch of flowers and kissed my hand. Blushing with embarrassment I took my seat.

I liked the music very well, but I should have preferred to listen to it without company. Fritz held my hand all the time and kissed it constantly. That was very bothersome. During the intermissions we spoke about the opera. I pretended that I had heard this opera several times and knew every singer. I answered a certain question with: "The singer doesn't seem to be well disposed to-day."

After the performance Fritz made a proud declaration of love and asked how I thought our relations were going to be in the future. I answered: "My nature is pretty cool. You'll see that."

I decided to shake him off as soon as possible. Hans and Olga did not get along very well together. I there-

YES! BUT—

fore tried to talk him into another girl friend of mine, Elsa. I called his attention to the fact, however, that she was more or less engaged to another fellow. But if he, Hans, did not proceed too stupidly, it would be quite easy to estrange her from her boy friend who, by the way, was a disagreeable chap.

Elsa was just giving a party to several of her friends, when I came in with my two boys. During a game of forfeits Hans wanted to give me a kiss. However I was already disgusted with him to such a degree that I refused to let him kiss me. All the others made a fuss about that for the other girls kissed their boys without ado. The most I granted him was permission to kiss my hand—and even that with reluctance. They called me affected, which I really was at that time. I spoke affectedly, turned continuously from one side to the other and said on every occasion: "That is much too low for me!"

On the way home I informed Hans that Elsa had invited us to her birthday party. If he wanted to wheedle himself into her good graces he probably would have to make her a present. At my suggestion he bought her a manicure set.

Elsa was really surprised at the generosity of my boy friend—in general he was considered as such. Between him and me, however, there existed merely a friendship, only that Hans did everything I wanted him to do.

245

THE CASE OF MISS R.

I did not allow him to bring the obtrusive Fritz along this time.

After a little while Hans complained to me that Elsa did not seem to be interested in him. He could not get any farther with her.

Then I went to her to sound her out about him. She answered very reservedly. While we were talking she combed her hair. Suddenly the thought occurred to me to take a wisp of her hair that had come out in combing and bring it to Hans. I do not know myself why I was so eager to procure a girl for him.

The tendency to play the matchmaker is distinctly based on the malicious intention to harm, which we can also notice on other occasions. Her intrigues are always intended to injure girls, her rivals.

When he came to me the next time, I gave him the hair in an envelope and said: "Elsa sends you this as a souvenir." At the same time I gave him the strict injunction not to speak about it to her because she did not wish it.

Thereupon Hans conceived new hope and began to court Elsa again.

But when I noticed that she was in love with her fool the whole business started to annoy me. I decided not to see her any more and instructed Hans; "Leave that silly girl alone! You come along with me now to another one!"

YES! BUT—

And I brought him to Walli, a girl whom I knew through Elsa. I talked to him so long until he told her he loved her and begged her for a kiss.

A long time afterwards Hans came to us one day and said to me, smiling peculiarly, that he did not feel quite well. I went out with him for a while and, on my insistent questioning, he finally confessed to me that he had contracted gonorrhea. He added, "A real man of the world must have such a thing." Although I thought his disease very interesting I avoided giving him my hand for fear of infection.

Obvious fear of infection, probably used for the purpose of eliminating the problem of love.

Furthermore I found out that he had stolen some of his mother's jewelry and had taken it to a pawn-broker. He had also stolen money from his father's safe. The result was that, from now on, his parents were very strict with him; he was allowed to go out only on Sunday afternoon. Then he called for me, and we merely took a walk.

My father liked Hans very much and was amused when I told him that it was the boy's greatest ambition to be a man of the world. In the black suit which father had made for him the little fellow really looked quite good. . .

One Sunday afternoon I went with Olga to the city park. Young as I was, my parents gave me every

THE CASE OF MISS R.

freedom. We strolled up and down in front of the music pavilion. Two naval officers came along, looked and smiled at us. Olga and I blinked at each other, turned our heads slowly around and saw that the two men were following us. And suddenly they addressed us. We were so embarrassed that we could hardly answer. We had met with many an adventure with young fellows before; but young men like these, that was something entirely new. My companion introduced himself to me and started to relate stories about life at sea. In order to make ourselves more interesting, we pretended to be foreigners—Olga was a Hungarian and I a Rumanian—and spoke broken German. We could not, however, maintain the deception. Our embarrassment threw us into still greater confusion—we were timid anyway. We grew more and more silent, the two men almost had to pull every word from our lips. But my naval officer seemed to be very pleased with my timidity. He never took his eyes off me, showed me every courtesy and inquired interestedly about my home conditions. Olga also blushed continuously and did not quite know what to reply. Then we went to a café. Gradually we became more lively. Time passed by in cheerful conversation. We were startled when the clock struck seven. The officers brought us to the trolley station. They would have liked to bring us home but we de-

YES! BUT—

clined this offer for reasons of decency. My officer, who had not ceased his attentions to me, emphasized how he regretted that this was the last day of his leave of absence and that he had to return to port the following day. He begged me to come to the railroad station. Since I did not know whether Olga or another girl would have time to go with me and I was afraid to go alone I made up some excuse. Then he wanted to have my address in order to write to me. I replied that he must not write to me at home, but I gave him the address of Olga's brother who was serving his apprenticeship in another shop. When he said goodbye to me my new admirer was quite moved; he admonished me to be good and promised to be back soon. "Little girl" he called me. Again he declared it a pity that he had not met me sooner. He would never forget me, he said. Would I permit him to address me by my first name? Once in a while I was to think of him. There were tears in his eyes when he pressed my hands. I remained completely unmoved. It only seemed strange to me that a man who sees a girl for the first time can fall so deeply in love.

Two weeks passed. I had gradually forgotten our meeting. One day Olga came to our house and whispered to me that I should come with her immediately because she had several letters and postcards which had accumulated at her brother's place. At

THE CASE OF MISS R.

first I was very much surprised. Then I was happy, if only for the fact that the other officer, in spite of his promise, had not written to Olga.

The letters were extremely tender. For that reason they caused unpleasant sensations in me. While reading them a trembling came over me. I felt urged to something that was against my nature. I presumed that he wanted to chain me to himself, which roused my indignation to such an extent that I was restless all day long. I was still almost a child. I had not even had my period yet. The mere thought of having to be alone with a man horrified me. I sat down in my bedroom and imagined what would happen to me if I were his wife. This made me angry with him and disgusted with myself.

Distinct expression of evasion of love.

Olga advised me to answer, but in a cool manner. And then we talked about that certain thing which he surely would demand. We started to ridicule him, and I sneered: "If he thinks I am going to kiss him, he'll have to wait a long time." I had never kissed before. A kiss alone seemed to be the worst. Then I received a letter or a postcard from him almost daily. He also sent me his photograph. At last he inquired whether, on his next sojourn in Vienna, he might propose to me. That disquieted me still more. The thought of being torn from my accustomed surroundings was

YES! BUT—

unbearable. I made an evasive and short answer. My parents, who did not object to such an advantageous marriage, teased me when they noticed my embarrassment. I said to my father, "I will only marry you."

Psychoanalysts of the Freudian school would regard this remark as proof that the sexual desires of this girl are directed toward her father. It would be an example of this girl's Œdipus complex, upon which Freud later laid less stress. However, we have long seen from the context that there is no possibility of a sexual relation between her and her father; for her, her father is asexual. Not every desire of a girl is a sexual desire or concerns itself with sexuality (libido). But every wish is a wish to rise, to win more power and security, to improve one's situation and position in the community. When sexuality shows itself a suitable means for this purpose, it is adapted to the striving for power and serves as a weapon to achieve success. We do not believe sexuality to be the primal urge, neither for the beginning nor for the end, but believe it to be a means which one uses as necessity arises, but which one can abandon as easily as one resorts to it, when other ways lead to the goal.

The father of this girl is a comparatively weak man. She knows that she can rule him. *I will only marry father* means in the language of her system: "I want to rule father, I alone and as completely as possible."

251

THE CASE OF MISS R.

Her first acquaintance with marriage led her to believe that it was a battle ground on which one loses or wins. She is reasonably sure of her victory so she wants to proceed on *that* battlefield where she has no defeat to dread and refuses to make one step on another field which she does not know and where she may experience defeat.

I was still pretty childish.

The naval officer did not abandon his suit. In one of his next letters he informed me that one of his comrades would come to see me in his name. That terrified me again. Moreover, we were not in a position to receive an officer in our apartment. We did not even have one room where one could talk alone to a person. Every corner was crowded with father's tailoring business.

In the meantime we had often talked about putting me into an office.

She will now be brought face to face with the great, human problem of work or vocational occupation. She has solved most incompletely the two other great social problems, social contact and love. Our expectations are not very high, but we are most interested to see what she will do with the question of work. As a pampered child she will also be badly prepared for this problem of life and will hesitate, stop or run away.

252

YES! BUT—

After finishing business school I did not do any work at all. I got up at ten in the morning, demanded food at once and ate an awful lot. All day long I visited friends and only came home for meals. Father was of the opinion that it could not go on like that any longer; I could either help a little at home or else get a job in an office. Household work did not interest me in the least. In an office I could make some money. So, one morning, father looked through the newspaper and found an advertisement inserted by a chemical factory for an office girl.

Mother and I went out to the plant. They engaged me right away.

Then we rode to Lina who was at the hospital. My sister was on night duty, so we could speak to her during the day, otherwise I should not have seen her any more before starting my new job. In the trolley car I could see from my mother's face that she had something on her mind. She sat silently beside me. Soon she confessed that she would rather see me refuse the position; the factory was too far from home; it would be too much of a rush for me.

When Lina heard the news, she embraced and kissed me and gave me plenty of advice on my conduct. Then we went home.

Father also seemed to regret his idea. He probably did not think that I should get a job so easily. He, too, was of the opinion that the location of the office was

THE CASE OF MISS R.

too far from home. And what is more I had continuous working hours with only one-half hour for lunch. I would not be able to stand it, he said. He was quite excited. But I insisted on trying at least. "First you chase me out of the house," I reproached him, "and then you want to stop me."

The next morning I woke up very early. Mother helped me dress. Then she gave me a thermos-bottle with hot tea, cold pork, bread and a few lumps of sugar. Father blessed me as if I were going on a long journey and told me to come home if there was anything I did not like. My parents were both quite upset. In a rather depressed mood I started.

She probably expects great honor from her job. According to the usual nature of such office positions we may assume that this girl will soon find her way back to her parents. The excitement of which she speaks indicates the intense tension into which such people are thrown who do not think of the work they are going to do nor of other persons, but solely of their triumph or possible defeat. In this increased tension the aforementioned stage fright originated as a sign of a poorly developed social feeling and an exaggerated interest in one's own person. At the same time courage, self-confidence, and an optimistic attitude can be found only among individuals who feel that they are in contact with other human beings and at

YES! BUT—

home with them. Courage is the result of a perfect social feeling.

A few old maids were working in the office. My first task was to rule lines in a large note book. I was so excited that I made a few ink spots in it. Then I had to file copies alphabetically. That hurt my eyes.

Her intense interest in her eyes, probably fostered by her parents—she was near-sighted and was frequently admonished to take care of her eyes—breaks through as a signal for retreat.

The manager of the office was a young man in uniform. He took me into his office, showed me around, encouraged me, and said that, of course, everything was new the first day but that I would soon be accustomed. However, I had had enough already from what I had seen so far.

During my lunch time I ate the bread and cold pork and drank the tea. But that was as good as nothing. I was used to devouring tremendous portions, several plates of soup and so on, reading all the time I ate. The old maids made me nervous, too. All of a sudden I got severe abdominal cramps. I went to the ladies' room and had to keep going there all afternoon.

It is only an assumption and would have to be confirmed by other facts that this girl belongs to the type

THE CASE OF MISS R.

which reacts to increased psychical tension by gastro-intestinal disturbances.

Later on I broke the thermos bottle. And then it was five o'clock at last. I staggered exhausted to the trolley car.

At home each member of my family surpassed the other in pitying me. Lina took me in her arms and sighed: "Poor child, you have had to work so hard!" Mother also embraced and kissed me. Father descended from his sewing table, stroked me, looked lovingly into my eyes and kissed my forehead. Then mother cooked a delicious meal, all my favorite dishes. But I was so exhausted that I could not eat. That made father excited. "Don't you see," he exclaimed, "she'll break down? If she goes to this office for only a few days, I'll have her lying here sick in bed! How she looks! Pale, drawn cheeks! She can't stand that! She needs an office where there are many young girls, where she isn't watched so closely, where she doesn't have to work so hard and has a little time to amuse herself, an office that isn't so far from here! She isn't going to go there again!"

Her attitude incites the pampering group to help her in her intention to give up her position. The retreat is complete.

Just as we finished our dinner the bell rang. Mother and Lina went to open the door. From the kitchen I

256

YES! BUT—

heard the voice of a man whom I did not know. Lina came back to the kitchen. It was the friend of the naval officer. I was startled. I did not feel like saying two words to him and therefore asked my sister to pretend that I had gone out. In a way I was sorry. However, since I was still weak from the abdominal pain of the afternoon I was afraid of making a bad impression. And, besides, the whole affair annoyed me.

Evasion from love and possible marriage. We must not be surprised or become dubious when we notice that she is trying to attain her goal with sound reasons. Such reasons are often used merely as an alibi; or something occurs that is evaluated as a strong counter-reason. If we are certain of our interpretation, the counter-reasons are not so important. We do not see any positive act which would lead to the solution of the love problem.

Mother and Lina talked to the officer for a while. I did not move. When he had gone I slipped into my bed completely exhausted. I could hear father say to mother that she should let me sleep as long as I wanted, so that I could recuperate from the hardships of the day. Then I fell asleep.

The next morning father went to the office to give notice on the pretext that I was sick. When he asked for my papers the manager did not give them to him, but said I should come back to the office as soon as I

THE CASE OF MISS R.

*felt better. However, father forbade me to go there.
After two weeks I received my papers back. I received
only one more letter from the naval officer written
in a sad mood. Thereafter I did not hear from him any
more. . . .*

*One day I went shopping downtown with a girl
friend of mine. Two young officers addressed us on the
street. We refused to talk to them; but that did not
discourage them and they inveigled us in a conversation. I went on ahead with one of them and lost sight
of the other two. The young lieutenant led me through
narrow, quiet streets. It was evening. All of a sudden
he seized me and wanted to kiss me. I resisted with all
my might. He tore my veil, which I had borrowed
from Lina. I was furious and cried: "Now you leave
me alone right away!" He grew pale and apologized.
I replied that I did not want to have anything to do
with him and that I did not care to see him any longer.
He said he had torn my veil and would compensate.
I refused any compensation and walked away. He
came after me, apologized again and threatened to give
the money for the veil to a beggar unless I gave him
my address. I told him to do as he pleased and again
left him. But he followed right on my heels and talked
and talked to me until I relented and even agreed to
make an engagement with him. In order to show off
with an officer I decided to meet him in our neighborhood. But when I saw him waiting on the square with*

YES! BUT—

a bunch of roses in his hand I felt embarrassed. I carried the roses bashfully with their heads down.

The justified repulse of a too aggressive officer (who certainly had a right to expect more of girls who permitted themselves to be accosted on the street) is followed by her making an engagement with him in order to show him off to her acquaintances. That illustrates again how she evades the challenge of love, how she misuses it to feed her vanity, which is nothing more than her longing to appear more than she really is.

He proposed going to a café. At first I did not want to. But since it was quite chilly, I went in with him. While we were talking, he asked me if I would not rather be alone with him. I answered that no one was disturbing us anyway. Then he said he did not mean it that way, it was so uncomfortable here, he would like to be all alone with me. Now I understood. "What do you mean? You can't have me for that! I want to go home!" He seemed indignant. We left the café.

On the street he tried to persuade me again and asked if I were afraid of him. He gave me his word of honor as an officer that he would not do me any harm. And while we were walking along he suddenly tried to push me into a house—I believe it was a hotel. I ran away. He came after me. When he caught up with me, I screamed at him furiously that he could not

THE CASE OF MISS R.

force me to do anything he wanted, that I had never been alone with a man and had no desire to be either. "Is that so? You don't believe what I say!" he shouted back. "That is an insult! I have given you my word of honor! I am not a scamp! Think it over, please!"

"I have nothing to think over. Don't fool yourself!"

Finally, after much coaxing, I made another engagement with him. This time he brought his photograph. That, I thought, was silly. We rode to a park. There he asked me at once to kiss him. I said to him: "Now, look here. I have never kissed a man, and if I ever should do it, then only for love. But I am not in love with you."

"For that you don't have to be in love. You'll learn how to fall in love with me, just wait. Probably you don't even know what a real kiss is."

That made me curious. I thought it might be a shame not to know what a real kiss was like, and decided not to withstand him, in case he should try to steal one from me. I did not have to wait long until he gave me a kiss. But I only felt disgusted. Then I said to him that I was cold and wanted to go home. He was obviously offended that his kiss had not made me warm instead of cold, and shouted at me in an angry voice: "Either—or! Either I shall never see you again or we shall love each other, which you certainly will not have to repent. Didn't I give you my word of

YES! BUT—

honor as an officer? What on earth do you think I am?"

"With that sort of voice you don't get anywhere with me. I will not—that settles it."

"Think it over! I'll give you a week's time! And if you don't agree, return my picture."

"Your picture—there it is. Take it! Goodbye!"

I handed it to him, turned around and went off.

Early the next day I ran over to Tilda, told her that I had been kissed and that I knew at last what a real kiss was. I described in detail all sorts of delight which I had not felt at all. And then I advised her to obtain the same pleasure for herself as soon as possible.

We see her approaching the terminus of her relations to the other sex by which she is afraid of being defeated. She no longer has any fear about being the first one. She only wants to play with fire. Immediately after she boasts to Tilda and tries to make her go over the dangerous road which she herself abominates.

The evening after the kiss I washed my mouth out thoroughly with potassium permanganate and spit out ten times. . . .

Tilda had a friend with whom she was quite deeply in love. That vexed me. I tried to incite her against him, I endeavored to persuade her that he was not suited to her. I did not succeed with this method, so I called on Minna for assistance and suggested that she

THE CASE OF MISS R.

should make some disparaging remarks about him to Tilda. So she said to Tilda: "My, that boy is a homely fellow!" Tilda replied scornfully: "I don't care if you like him or not—as long as I like him."

This endeavor to disturb others in their love happiness expresses her general aversion to love and, at the same time, her inclination to be a marplot when she is not the center of attention. Spoiled children who do not lead in class-work or games act similarly in school by disturbing the others since they feel incapable of obtaining the leading rôle.

What follows is an attempt to make a joke out of the love play, which is too dangerous to her ambition; by fooling men, she preserves her feeling of superiority over them.

In order to change Tilda's ideas I took her out with me every afternoon. We put on large hats and pressed them down on our faces. A fur which father had made for me covered my face up to the eyes. Tilda did the same with a fox fur. One could see nothing of our faces but the eyes which we rolled crazily when we met a man. We were frequently addressed by men who took us to cafés; there we devoured a lot of pastry and afterward made our escape. One day an elderly gentleman between forty and fifty addressed us and invited us to a barroom. That was something new. At first we hesitated, but as were two against

YES! BUT—

one we thought that nothing could happen to us. An elaborately dressed woman with bleached hair received us, whispered a few words in the gentleman's ear and showed us to a little booth with a curtain in front of it. The gentleman ordered wine. We began to feel alarmed. The curtain, however, was not drawn. Except for a piano-player, who was just starting to play a dance, no other person was in the restaurant. The wine had scarcely been poured into the glasses, when Tilda whispered to me that I should be careful because the man might perhaps have put some narcotic or exciting drug into the wine. That sufficed to terrify me.

Although we were constantly urged to drink, we only took small sips of the wine. We made up instead on the cookies. The man then took a seat between us. We receded anxiously. I had already repented having accepted the invitation and was wondering how we could manage to get away as soon as possible. The man did not look as if he could be easily fooled. He was angry because we withdrew from him and asked in an irritated tone what we were supposed to be here for. We became more and more dejected. When he left the room for a moment, we wanted to use the opportunity to get out. We deliberated on what to do in case he attempted to rape us. There were no weapons, of course, with which we could have defended ourselves. Tilda had the idea of attacking him

THE CASE OF MISS R.

in case of need with the two empty chairs beside us. In order to be prepared in time we laid our hands on the arm-rest. After coming back he started to sidle up to us. We repulsed him again. He became furious, called us silly kids, impertinent dumb-bells, and accused us of having cheated him. That was very disagreeable to us. He renewed his advances. But we succeeded in pushing him away without the assistance of the chairs. Finally nothing remained for him to do but to pay. The lady with the yellow hair looked dumbfounded when she saw him leave the place without having effected his purpose. On the street the man swore at us again. But now we felt safe; we told him to go to hell and marched off. We were glad to have gotten away with a mere fright and decided to be a little more careful the next time.

Lina induced me to take dancing lessons twice a week. I let a different boy take me home each time. But I never kissed one of them. One day Tilda came to me with another girl and told me that there was going to be a masquerade in our neighborhood. The three of us could go in old-fashioned Viennese costumes.

I was delighted at this idea, all the more so since I had never attended a ball. I agreed at once, although I did not know how to arrange about getting out. Father had always opposed my going to dances and balls on account of my poor health. And I had no

YES! BUT—

suitable dress and by no means the money to buy a new costume. Tilda and Gretel had prepared their white dresses and black masks, whereas I had not yet had the courage to tell father about it. At the last moment, I resolved to ask a rich girl whom I knew to lend me a dress and whatever else I needed for the ball. She agreed, and I picked from her numerous dresses one that seemed to be best suited for the ball. She also let me have a mask and a little fan; patent leather shoes I had myself. I told father that I was going to see Tilda; I had let mother into the secret. She also gave me the money to buy a ticket.

Tilda had already left for the ball when I came to her house with my parcel, containing, among other things, some powder and a lipstick from Lina. Tilda's mother helped me dress. But since the rich girl whose dress I was going to wear was about three times as stout as I, her dress was far too wide for me. We had to pin it together hastily with safety-pins. Then I tried on the mask. It pressed against my face and screwed up my eyelids. However, there was no more time to adjust it. When I mounted the stairs to the ballroom I noticed that all the other girls came in accompanied by men. Only I was alone, which troubled me a little. For that reason I put on the mask. But I had to lift it several times in order not to stumble.

The dance floor was packed. There was an intermission just when I entered. I searched for my friends

THE CASE OF MISS R.

and soon found them. They were sitting on a bench whispering to one another. I took a seat beside them, but they did not recognize me. After a while I bent over to Tilda and said; "How do you do, Miss Tilda." Both girls were quite perplexed and then very glad I had been able to come. The music began to play, we were asked to dance and danced incessantly. We had paid for our tickets, but unfortunately possessed not one more penny to buy something to eat or drink. And we were both hungry and thirsty.

A gentleman with quite a bourgeois appearance asked me for a dance. He looked much too old for me, had a funny pronunciation and did not dance very well. However, I was in hopes that he would help me quench my thirst and so I talked to him after the dance for a while. Then I introduced him to my friends. Before that, I had whispered to Tilda; "Listen, I have caught a fish who can't even dance decently. But I hope he takes us to the restaurant. You two must flirt with him."

The gentleman did not seem to be exceedingly delighted suddenly to have three girls with him instead of one. But I made him understand, either all three—or none! Thus the four of us went to the restaurant and drank wine.

After a quarter of an hour, I asked him to excuse me and left the dancing gentleman to my girl friends. He soon followed me and wanted to dance

YES! BUT—

with me continuously. I escaped whenever I could.

A large cap was suspended from the ceiling at one end of the hall. The couple that happened to pass under the cap during a dance had to get "married"; that is, they had to kiss each other in a separate room. Most unfortunately I danced under the cap with the old man. But I refused to let him kiss me. I said; "I'll send you my girl friend, Tilda. I don't want to." Tilda in turn referred him to Gretel, who did not want to do it either. Thus the poor man was done out of a kiss and had incurred expenses for nothing.

Afterwards I danced eagerly and received many flowers in little bunches. I fled from one man to another. Only the mask disturbed me. I was glad when midnight came and I could take it off. Now I danced all the more; I made several engagements with men but I did not keep one of them. And then the ball was over. Several young chaps asked if they might take us home. We refused politely.

I dressed in Tilda's house. Her mother laughed at our experience with the poor fish, as we called him. Then I went home. Father was still awake. He made an angry face when he saw me. I did not let him get a word in edgewise, and told him so many funny stories about the ball that he could not help laughing. At last he only said; "You are never to go alone to a ball. The next time I'll go with you if I have time. Dancing all night and then expecting others to pay for you."

THE CASE OF MISS R.

I always had to wear one and the same dress for my dancing lessons. For a long time I had wanted to get a new one. But we never had money enough to buy one. I thought my head off trying to find a way to manage to make a little money. Of course, I did not want to be chained to an office. I simply hated office work.

Every now and then I looked through the advertisements in our newspaper. One day I happened to see the following advertisement; "Help wanted. Easy work. Good pay, etc." I showed this advertisement to my parents. They did not like the idea of my taking such a job. They asked what good it had done to send me to business school. I replied that I cared only to make some money; how I earned it made no difference to me.

The next day I was already sitting at a long table, stripping feathers apart. The other women looked at me with curious eyes. But I did not take any notice of them and stripped my feathers mechanically. Much dust was caused by this work which continually irritated my throat. I had to cough a lot. I tried to combat the cough by thinking of the money that I would earn and the dress that I would buy for it. Then I remembered a moving picture in which an assistant worker like me married the boss. Unfortunately my boss was a small, old man with a paunch. When I told father about my debut as a feather-stripper, he said the job was no good for me because it would endanger

268

YES! BUT—

my lungs. I went there once again. Then father forbade it. I got my few cents and decided to look for another position.

I thought I had found the right one when, after some time, I read the following advertisement: "School for moving picture actresses. Professor N. N." This time Lina had to accompany me. We were received by the alleged professor, who still looked quite young, in a room decorated with red wall-paper and a grand piano. He asked us to attend a rehearsal first. After that he would examine me.

Two young men and a very gay young woman came in and rehearsed a love scene. Then it was my turn. One of the men was to be my partner and was to represent my father, who objected to my being married. The young man immediately commenced making grimaces. I played the sad one. And then I imagined how I acted when father denied me a wish. I stamped my feet on the floor and bawled: "Don't be so nasty!" Every one began to laugh; they all applauded and cried: "Excellent." The Professor thought I had much talent and wanted to arrange to give me lessons at once. But Lina told him that she had to talk to our parents first. When father heard about the new plan he was dubious about its value. Moreover, it was impossible for him to procure the fee for lessons. Thus this career also found its premature end.

THE CASE OF MISS R.

A little later on the idea came to my mind to become assistant to a dentist such as Lina had been. I thought this sort of work pretty easy. Besides, I was curious to see how people behaved when they had a tooth pulled. Soon I found an advertisement in the paper and applied as nurse in a dentist's office. The dentist, an elderly man with whiskers, did not please me. He asked me if I had had any previous experience and I had to answer in the negative. Then he murmured something, put down my name and address in his note-book, and dismissed me.

Two days later I got a postcard from him asking me to come to see him. Before he decided to engage me, he asked me at length about my family and other personal details. He seemed to be a pedantic man. Then his wife came in and looked me over. She wore a dressing gown. It was most repugnant to me to have to shake hands with her. In addition to the tiny salary, he promised me plentiful tips. He also told me that my predecessor had gotten married. The last thing he did was to caution me always to have my hair neatly combed.

The following morning I had to be at his office at half past seven. The dentist showed me the most important of his instruments, explained how to fix the drill, etc. My head ached from seeing so many instruments. In came the first patient. I took a place at her left, covered her neck with a small towel, and put

YES! BUT—

water in a glass. The dentist lit the little spirit flame and pumped hot air on the tooth. I had to heat a tiny mirror over the flame so that it would not become misty from the patient's breath. I was so excited I held the mirror over the flame too long, and suddenly my chief cried; "Enough! Otherwise the mirror will crack." My old fear of mirrors came over me like lightning. I could see the little mirror cracked and myself burdened with seven years of misfortune. And at the same time I reflected upon how to get away. Besides, I disliked very much the rubber plate which served to isolate the tooth under treatment and dripped with saliva.

At first sight the frequent change of occupation seems to be justified, but we may assume that it will be difficult for this girl to find a suitable position as long as she does not change her style of life. In the dentist's office her whole attention is directed toward finding a way of escape. The old, apparently forgotten fears of mirrors comes in at the right time. *Besides, I also felt a strong dislike.* The famous "besides" in a neurosis.

Finally I had to carry out the brass pot into which the patient spit, and sterilize the instruments. All this and the obnoxious odor of my hands sickened me to such a degree that I could hardly eat anything for lunch.

THE CASE OF MISS R.

At two o'clock I had to be back. Then the dentist showed me how to wind absorbent cotton around a nerve needle and advised me to practice that thoroughly. His wife appeared again, saying I was to help her mend the linen when I had some time. I thought to myself: "You can wait a long time. What else? All day long on my feet and in addition, mend her laundry."

Now the parade of patients began. However, I was cheated of the spectacle that I wanted to see most of all; no one had a tooth pulled.

Persons who feel inferior and weak are always interested in being present at the misfortune of others. Some children train and practice to be cruel because they are ashamed of their weakness. They stand around shivering when a pig is slaughtered but the spectacle nevertheless attracts them over and over again. They intend to harden themselves, they read continually or listen to ghost stories, and so on. The accomplished tyrant is always cowardly and a weakling as well.

I finished my work with difficulty. In the evening I went home and never returned to the office.

CHAPTER XII

THE GOAL OF SUPERIORITY

ONE day, while we were taking a walk, Tilda's friend pulled her onto a gutter drain and held her on it. Both shook with laughter. Surprised, I asked them what that meant. Tilda answered: "Don't you know that one doesn't get a husband if one stands on a gutter drain?" I cocked my ears at once and thought: "Peculiar. I always disliked stepping on one of these gutter drains, sort of a dull presentiment that it would mean mischief!" Now I believed I had found out at last what was behind that feeling. Afraid of being pushed or pulled onto a gutter drain like Tilda with the result of never being able to acquire a husband, I went out with them quite reluctantly from that time on.

Again a new compulsion idea. You see that the symptoms change like the colors of a chameleon, adjusting themselves along neurotic lines to changing environment and conditions. The chameleon, the neurosis, remains the same. Even if the symptoms were to disappear temporarily (and on closer inspec-

THE CASE OF MISS R.

tion there would be enough neurotic signs to discover) that would be no guarantee for the disappearance of the neurosis. What it signifies is that the neurosis, for the time being, needs fewer alarming symptoms or does not consider them necessary. Patients often overlook that fact when they believe themselves to be quite cured because they have been temporarily freed of their troublesome symptoms. Symptoms are small parts, but we are interested in the whole human being. A criterion for a cure lies alone in how the entire individual reacts in the future to life and to the demands life makes of him.

This girl goes further, step by step, in her compulsion neurosis. One restriction follows another and each is more complete, more comprehensive. The construction of her neurosis is throughout intelligent and consistent. From which one can see that even the intelligence is nothing but an instrument to be used either in overcoming life's obstacles, or in evading them, depending upon the goal set.

The reason for her reluctance was probably due to the fact that she did not feel that she was the center of the situation. The gutter drain idea could free her of the fatal thought of being superfluous, or one among many. This shows why the logical arguments and explanations of her friends cannot help the patient. The gutter drain idea has another purpose than to be logically discussed, and the idea is perfectly

THE GOAL OF SUPERIORITY

correct and intelligent in the light of this other purpose. Private intelligence against common sense. We find this form of private intelligence throughout the reflections of all kinds of persons with conduct disorders, such as problem children ("because I don't want to . . ."), neurotics as in the present case, insane people ("because I am influenced by electric currents"), criminals ("because he has better clothes than I"), suicides ("because life has no meaning"), perverts ("because perversions are a higher form of love culture"), drunkards, morphinists ("because I cannot live without these remedies"), superstitious people ("because something brings good luck or bad luck") and so on. All are justifications to the attainment of personal goals, but not one considers the general, human purpose of the community. And that is why they all belong in a neurotic system.

Soon I could do nothing but believe in the mysterious connection between a gutter drain and its various consequences. Even if I could have been furnished with clear proof that this remark of Tilda's was merely a silly saying—Finni, a friend of Lina's, whom I had repeatedly seen stepping on gutter drains, got married in spite of it—even then no one could have changed my mind any more. My friends wondered why I made a big detour around the gutter drains or became frightened when I saw one. When

THE CASE OF MISS R.

they asked me why I avoided them so carefully, I answered: "Why, they stink so badly. I can't stand the smell."

One day, when we passed a gutter drain and I had shown my usual signs of fright, I explained to a young man how my fear originated. He placed himself on a gutter drain before my eyes and stood there for a while. That seemed so funny to me that I had a fit of laughter. At the same time I felt sorry for him. I said to myself: "Now he can wait a long time until he gets a wife." There was no doubt in my mind as to the truth of this superstition.

I noticed that there was a gutter drain near the trolley station where I had to get off. I immediately re-entered the car and got off at the next station. Another day I arrived at the same station with a girl who knew that we had to get off there. I did not see any other way out of my dilemma but to jump over the drain. In spite of this precaution I imagined I had touched the drain with my foot. I became very despondent, said good-bye to the girl and went straight home. I told my parents that something terrible had happened to me. They were terrified. But when they heard what had happened they became almost hysterical with laughter. Father put on his overcoat and promised to show me that he would step on a gutter drain a hundred times. I answered, sobbing, that this was not the same in his case since he already had a

THE GOAL OF SUPERIORITY

wife and therefore did not have to be afraid any more. It would be different if Lina were to do it. So my sister really placed herself on a gutter drain right in front of me. But that did not quiet me. On the contrary, I cried all the more, reproaching myself with the thought that if Lina did not get a husband I should be guilty.

It was often only necessary for me to be near a gutter drain to start the fixed idea that I had somehow touched it. Only when I had succeeded in inducing all my friends, one after the other, to step on the drain, without letting them know what I was aiming at, did I feel somewhat relieved. But when winter came and the streets were covered with snow, I only dared to venture out with the most elaborate precautions. I was continually on the watch for gutter drains covered by snow. One evening I felt as if I had stepped on one. I ran home in a frenzy of despair, crying and raving. Then I returned to the spot where the accident had happened, to find out whether there really was a gutter drain. There was none at all, only a puddle.

The fear of gutter drains made going out almost impossible for me. I had examined my own neighborhood very carefully to see where all the drains were located; but further out there were innumerable, unknown, spiteful gutter drains. In spite of my apprehensiveness about going around with men, the

THE CASE OF MISS R.

prospect of having to remain an old maid for the rest of my life seemed to me the most despicable fate. "Old maid"—the mere name terrified me. In sheer desperation the idea came to me to retreat from this world and enter a cloister.

This fear of gutter drains places all responsibility for possible failure to find a husband on the drain, and leaves her personal attractiveness intact. Her vanity and pride are saved. If no one wants her it is the fault of the gutter drain, just as it was before the fault of the broken mirror. Similar superstitions are frequent among children who make certain acts responsible for failure in schoolwork; as, for example, stepping on the dividing lines between sidewalk squares, leaping over a number of stairs, and so on.

Precisely taken, almost every human being can remember certain periods in his life when he had certain compulsion thoughts or felt forced to do certain things which led him into such difficulties. To illustrate: one man feels himself compelled to doubt everything he hears; another feels himself compelled, under certain circumstances or at certain hours of the day, to pray in order to maintain a mental balance; a third believes that he exists only by means of supernatural assistance and behaves as if everything were a present from this supernatural power. We see lighter forms of compulsion action in ordinary superstitions which compel the person concerned to do or not to do

THE GOAL OF SUPERIORITY

specific things; for instance, never to start a journey on Friday, never to light three cigarettes from the same match, never to put the left shoe or stocking on before the right, never to let a lamppost or similar street object come between him and his companion, and the like. Later on compulsion neuroses and phobias occasionally branch off from such traits.

These forms of childish superstition evidently disclose the existence of an aggravated inferiority feeling and the lack of confidence in one's own strength. Now and again, however, a successful attempt to busy oneself on the generally useful side of life can run parallel with the attempt to win laurels in the realm of superstition. Success in such cases is usually attributed to a fortunate omen. The patient, for instance, who suffered from the fixed idea that his sisters might burn to death if he did not pray for their safety from fire every night, saved his sisters not only from burning to death but he also constantly thought and took care of them, which was probably the deeper purpose of this fixed idea.

He was unconsciously forced to carry out his charitable intention and he would doubtlessly have been able to accomplish it consciously if the meaning of this unconscious compulsion had been made clear to him. The conscious and unconscious are not opposite poles, as Freud thinks; the passing over of thoughts into the unconscious is a means, a deception of the

THE CASE OF MISS R.

psyche which is always utilized when the personal feeling of integrity or the unity of the personality is threatened by some conscious misinterpretation.

In the course of this analysis we have frequently seen that this girl's psyche resorts to all sorts of artifices to overcome real and imaginary difficulties of life; to mention only her tendency to exaggerate or falsify happenings, her choice and purposive use of experience, and similar mechanisms. The nervous psyche is forced to make use of such tricks and artifices in order to be able even to approach the fictive, tension-producing goal. One of these artifices is the location of the goal in the unconscious, or the substitution of one neurotic goal for another in the unconscious. When there seems to be a stark contrast between the conscious and the unconscious (a fiction which the Freudian school has taken as truth), the difference is only in the means and has no significance in the final object of elevation of personality and the fictive goal of godliness.

We find this confirmed in the example of the man who prays for his sister's life. The conscious and unconscious pursue the same road, both guided by the goal of superiority on the useful side of life; that is to say, to take care of his sisters despite all obstacles.

Another trait in the gutter drain episode should be familiar to us. She feels relieved when her friends de-

THE GOAL OF SUPERIORITY

prive themselves of their chance of marrying by stepping on the drain.

My fear of gutter drains was supplemented by the following. One day I began to imagine that the trolley lines J and J2 would bring me misfortune. By and by I added to them the numbers 13, 3, 63, 43, and the letters A, Ak, B, Bk, D, and C, from the outskirts of the city to the center. It became absolutely impossible for me to use these lines. I often walked many blocks, even when the weather was bad. J and J2 were the most strictly forbidden cars—I do not use them up to the present. It can be seen that I had to face the worst difficulties on account of these prohibitions which I positively had to follow. I could tell many stories about my sufferings. One evening I got out of Car F at a crossing where I had to change to Car H. A car came along which I thought was Car H—I am somewhat near-sighted. I got in, sat down—all of a sudden I was surprised to notice that the supposed Car H ran straight down the "Loop" instead of turning into Alser Street. I jumped up, looked at the sign— what did I read? Car D. I rushed out and jumped off the car like one bereft of her senses. This mistake depressed me horribly. I believed I was going to have one misfortune after another from then on. Again I resolved to enter a cloister.

THE CASE OF MISS R.

We see how she restricts her radius of action by the car phobia and seeks, faced with the problem of love, for a way to avoid possible defeat by means of a cloister.

For the time being, however, I ironed the dress I had worn in that detested car in order to break the wicked spell. If I had been rich, I should have thrown away or burnt all the things I had had on, including my hairpins. But I, poor devil, had to be satisfied with ironing out that ill-fated dress, washing myself from head to foot and performing a counter-magic. I repeated a number three times.

Then it became quite impossible for me to go through certain streets. When I had to pass through one of them, I held my breath so that the air from it could not enter me and go down my throat. And if I had already breathed, I spat out three times and wiped my mouth with saliva. Which streets were they? I am still afraid to name them.

Lina used to be terribly angry when I dragged her along a street in a zig-zag, and constantly forced her to make detours.

The members of my family were also forbidden to ride in the cars with the unfortunate numbers, or walk through streets taboo for me. If I found out that they had done it anyway I did not let them come near me. I remembered with great care the clothes they had

THE GOAL OF SUPERIORITY

worn in those cars and streets and did not touch them again. And if I accidentally came in contact with them, I swore and fretted, tore off my dress and underwear, placed myself in front of the open window without a bit of clothing on in order to catch pneumonia and die, and finally threw myself in complete desperation on the bed.

The longing for death, closely related to suicidal tendencies, appears as a trial solution to escape defeat in the love problem. This is, as always, the effect of a tendency to exclude life when all other ways to a satisfactory solution of life's problems seem blocked. Instead of overcoming her difficulties by means of creative power and choice of a generally useful occupation, which would also help her to overcome her feeling of inferiority, she chooses to detach herself from and condemn the community and its offering, revenge herself on those who stand in her way, and acquire a fleeting feeling of superiority in experiencing mastery over her life and death. This is the confession of the weakling, of the hopeless.

The streetcar phobia, and the way this girl builds it up, again gives her power over her family, the weakest part in her environment.

I was once walking along a certain street and grazed a woman carrying a handbag. The idea suddenly struck me that she might live on one of those forbid-

THE CASE OF MISS R.

den streets. I followed her to see whether I was right or not, but eventually lost track of her.

I did not visit the moving picture theatres on that street any more. There might be people from forbidden streets in them. Not even a fine program could induce me. Then a number of coffee restaurants in different sections of the city became so repugnant to me that I closed my mouth and nose when I had to pass them. One day I forgot to protect myself in this manner in front of the Café Central. I remembered afterwards that I had passed this place and that from the revolving door of the Café had been blown a disastrous wind upon me. I felt as if I had been poisoned and turned about, raced home, flung my hat in a corner, tore off my clothing, cleaned my face with soap and water and washed out my mouth.

The streets abhorrent to me bred as rapidly as rabbits. There was already a whole district which I detested. When people from this forbidden district came to see us, I felt as if I were in a room with persons infected with the plague, whose mere breath brought ruin and who infected everything they touched. I would never use a chair on which one of them had sat. At last nothing remained for me to use but my own tattered and torn easy-chair which I guarded like a dragon. If some one showed the slightest intention of sitting on it I made a great fuss and prevented him. I dragged the chair with my own hands from the

284

THE GOAL OF SUPERIORITY

kitchen to the living room to use when I played the piano. My clothes were not allowed to be put on another chair.

One day mother was making hash. I was delighted in spite of the fact that it was horsemeat. While she was serving some of the hash to me, she accidentally brushed her arm against the armrest of a chair on which a forbidden person had been seated a short while before. I was furious and did not eat one bite of hash. That made mother so angry that she almost threw the whole pot on the floor.

It seems remarkable that even her love for the good midday meals her mother cooks cannot lessen her fear of uncleanliness. It might be thought that a strong desire, like one for physical pleasure, would have enough power to suppress at least temporarily her lust for power. That would be a superficial thought. Man is a unity. He does not consist of two or three wishes, fighting each other, with one or another conquering from time to time; he has only one goal and everything he does tends toward this goal. If, in the patient's opinion, physical pleasure can be used as a means toward this goal, such pleasure will be utilized or any other means which seems practical. But here the physical desire is interpreted as unimportant in her struggle toward her objective, superiority, so her desire is disregarded and secondarily

THE CASE OF MISS R.

made use of to illuminate her difficulties which make her struggle for superiority such an exhausting one. Our girl eats hash with great relish, and when she refuses to eat it, she regards her sacrifice as an heroic act and extracts an additional bit of superiority.

Plates, cups, forks and knives used by forbidden persons I never touched again. Mother had to stow away such utensils in another place apart from the rest of the pots and pans, so that I could always easily recognize them as untouchable for me. I grew accustomed to eating with knives, forks and spoons used only by me and had plates only for my use, just as during the time of my lupus phobia. If some one whom I did not like or any one of my family happened to touch one of my things after being contaminated by touching or using one of the obnoxious objects, I did not touch my things any more. Mother had to buy new implements.

One Saturday night something happened which "soiled" my special knife and fork. I immediately began to rave and scold mother because she had not been careful enough. The stores were already closed. It was impossible to buy me another set of eating utensils. Mother borrowed a fork from a neighbor.

To evade direct contact with all forbidden persons who came to the house I would withdraw to the bedroom. There I felt as if the evil eye which I ascribed

THE GOAL OF SUPERIORITY

to them penetrated the wall and brought misfortune upon me. So I went to bed and crept under the blankets.

When misfortune happens because of the evil eye, she herself is, of course, not responsible. The fault is laid to the evil eye. What is called bad luck in such cases is usually one's own mistakes and stupidities, the cause of which is sought somewhere outside instead of inside. The evil eye is one of those bugbears which would become a real danger for a neurotic only if it were absent or could not be resorted to.

Certain stores were also prohibited and mother was not allowed to shop in them. When I suspected that she had bought victuals in such a store, I cross-examined her, asked her the most cunning questions, set traps for her like a detective. And when I found out that she had lied to me, I swore at her in abusive language and behaved as if I had lost my head.

We remember that her use of abusive language began in her childhood (her first neurosis commenced with swearing). At that time she did it secretly and her conscience pricked her afterwards. Now she feels her swearing justified and does not bother to conceal it. It is obvious how the neurosis progresses.

After the slightest contact with forbidden persons or things I washed myself.

THE CASE OF MISS R.

We could have predicted that the last stage of this phobia would be a washing compulsion. Quite in contradistinction to the mentally defective, she proves her intelligence by choosing an intelligent plan for attaining her goal.

This girl appears superior again in the washing compulsion. She is the only pure human being in the world. Every one else is dirty. Again the parallelism between the conscious and the unconscious. Unconsciously the striving for power is a cheap way, customary among pampered children. Consciously an aversion to the dirt of others. The result is that the patient, without quite comprehending the full meaning of her actions, is the only one pure and superior. She would not deny it if one told her so but she would constantly reiterate and point to her torments. We understand: the more she is tormented by the dirt of others the purer she remains.

I frequently washed my whole body. I never used again a piece of soap which fell on the floor. My parents and Lina were not permitted to wash themselves with this cake of soap again. So the soap which had fallen on the floor accumulated and soon there was a pile of unusable soap.

I had a number of garments which I could no longer wear. I gave some of them to mother. But she was not allowed to come near me when she wore any of them.

THE GOAL OF SUPERIORITY

At home I wore an old, torn dress consisting of a green, worn-out skirt and a red blouse much too tight for me. I wore a pair of Bohemian slippers—if I could have managed it I should never have taken them off. Thus I sat like Cinderella in a corner of the kitchen on my broken chair with the rusty nails—in front of me all the things whose mere presence seemed pernicious to me, all the objects bewitched by the touch of residents of those execrated districts and streets, outside the gutter drains, streets, houses, gas lampposts, coffee restaurants, trolley cars, stores threatening with their wicked magic—danger, mischief, misfortune dogged my steps.

She describes her suffering with much skill and penetration. An antisocial, selfish life never leads to pleasure in the power which has been won over a few people at the expense of so much exertion. She sits like a tyrant on a throne which can be overturned at any moment; she rules by fear and is herself ruled by fear. She has to make her position in the "enemy country" secure by cunning and brute force. She has no real friends, no help, only oppressed subordinates who, she instinctively feels, would desert her if they could. No confidence, no candor, no love comes to her, only obscure mistrust, unwillingness of those she has made into servants, and dangerous counterpressure. The protecting measures which have been arranged for her own security prove themselves

289

THE CASE OF MISS R.

weapons in the hands of her enemies. The more she thinks of her security and how to preserve it the more insecure she becomes.

The suffering of the neurotic grows to an unbelievable torment and drives him into those great crises in which he either breaks down or hardens himself to the point where he becomes psychotic; or where he reaches the point of dim comprehension of the faulty construction of his unhappy struggle for recognition and then seeks enlightenment.

So-called logical arguments are of no avail in attempting to free this girl of her compulsion ideas and compulsion acts. She must be shown, step by step, the real construction of her behavior as we see it. She would have to learn to recognize what the purpose of her symptoms is and what she achieves thereby; that she wants unconsciously to detach herself by compulsion from the compulsion of communal demands; that she has built a secondary battlefield in her intense desire to avoid the principal battlefield of life; that she wants to fritter away her time so as to have none left for the accomplishment of her daily tasks; that she intends to evade life's demands with excuses, curses, alibis or ostensibly good reasons. In addition the erroneous views acquired in her childhood must be set aside, her exaggerated ambition and vanity, and the tendency to isolate herself must all be explained to her with great delicacy

THE GOAL OF SUPERIORITY

and tact. She can then be led to change her style of life by unmasking the technical apparatus of her compulsion neurosis and a clear understanding of the whole course and consistency of her conduct.

I started to menstruate unusually late. All my friends had started long ago. Olga, for example, had her period when she was fourteen. I remember that very well. One day she took my hand, while her eyes twinkled, led me into the bathroom, and suddenly lifted her skirts. I saw bloodstains on her bloomers. "What do you think of that?" she asked proudly. I was quite depressed and resolved to tell her in about two weeks that I was so far, too. Later on I always made my friends believe I had already begun menstruating. However year after year went by and the period did not set in.

It is likely that an innate inferiority of her sexual organs, for which there was apparently no compensation, was responsible for the retardation of her menstruation. This inferiority was probably indicated on other parts of her body.

My parents were quite worried and had me examined by a doctor. The doctor ordered hot seat-baths. At the age of seventeen the function finally set in. When I discovered the signs, I ran at once to father and told him. He embraced me happily and said; "Now you are a grown-up girl. You are no longer a

291

THE CASE OF MISS R.

*child. We must celebrate that." And my first men-
struation was celebrated by a good supper.*

*I frequently had a depressing dream. I dreamt that
father or mother was very sick. I woke up crying in
the middle of the night and burdened with a bad
conscience, and it took me a long time to fall asleep
again. And while I tossed in bed from one side to the
other I resolved to change myself, assist my parents
with their work, go on errands for father and help
mother with her housework.*

Almost all children dream occasionally of the death
or serious illness of one or the other of their parents.
To interpret such a dream by the saying "The wish is
father to the thought" is the privilege of a schematic,
insinuating psychology. On rare occasions this interpretation is correct. However, we shall make such a
decision only when the general mood of the dream
speaks for it and, most of all, when the behavior of
the dreamer otherwise justifies such an interpretation.
A mitigation of the death-wish can be found at such
times when, in spite of a strongly antagonistic attitude
toward the parents, such a dream passes off under
severe depression and sadness. This would be a sign
that the child's struggle against the parents does not
go so far as to wish for the parents' death.

What this dream usually does is attempt to foresee
the future— What is going to happen when my parents die?

THE GOAL OF SUPERIORITY

Permit me at this point to insert a few general remarks on the purpose and significance of dreams:

The dream is an obvious fiction in which a person arranges advance attempts and tests for controlling a future situation or solving a future problem. It is a fiction because an individual never views a dream situation in accordance with reality, but always transposes it as if it were reality and always as he would like to have it; he never really approaches reality, but tests his abilities under the influence of the dream and attempts a trial solution in it. A person dreaming is not different from a person awake; the only difference is in form of expression. In his waking life he occupies himself with the present, in dreams (daydreams or dreams in sleep) he busies himself with the future by means of the past, that is to say by his experiences. He constructs a fictive future out of the material of the past, out of his experiences. Dreaming he thinks in advance. And the way in which he thinks in advance mirrors graphically the psychic attitude of the dreamer, his courage, his adjustment to his environment, his character traits and their neurotic evasions, his own peculiar way of facing problems. The dream creates a mood whose purpose is to encourage or discourage the dreamer in approaching his problem. Such moods appear in all gradations from anxiety to indifference to outspoken courage. All the dreams of an individual are in accordance with his

THE CASE OF MISS R.

style of life; they belong to a system and are part of the individual unity. Conscious thought has little to do in a dream. The criticism and opposition of the sleeping sense organs are silenced. Thought in the dream is more abstract, simplified and symbolized—inclined toward a more childish state, as it were. The dream must remain unintelligible to the dreamer to protect the unity of his personality, to preserve the mood aroused in him, to veil the goal and direction of the dreamer in the unconscious.

There is not sufficient space here to explain more in detail the means used in dreams to accomplish their object—to a certain extent to explain the technique of dream interpretation. It will suffice to indicate that the dream, like every other soul manifestation, can be employed to gain insight into the psychic machinery of a human being.

It is evident in our case that the girl is anxious about her future. She needs her parents to be able to maintain a feeling of superiority. Although she emphasizes in the following paragraphs that the frequently recurring dream left no impression on the following day, the mood produced in the dream and its frequent repetition—a distinctly emotional training—has doubtless brought about an alleviation of her attitude toward her parents. This dream, therefore, signifies a certain amount of social feeling, interest in her parents.

THE GOAL OF SUPERIORITY

*In the morning, however, everything was forgotten
again. The day, the light, the morning blotted out my
feelings. At this time I had another tormenting worry.
I fancied I was extremely old. Sometimes I wondered
seriously whether it would not be best to end my life.
Then I said to myself: "The years are passing by so
quickly and misfortune approaches at a rapid pace."
I never told my true age. Such thoughts came to
me especially before falling asleep. Sometimes I woke
up frightened, my age flashed upon my mind and I
thought: "How wonderful it would be to be born
now!"*

So old, and nothing done yet for immortality!

The thoughts mentioned obviously touch the problem of love for which she does not feel prepared on
account of her exaggerated desire to rule. Then she
looks back at those ideal times when, in early childhood, the pampered girl actually possessed unlimited
power and did not have to face new problems.

*Father had had a weak heart for many years. At the
age of fifty-eight the malady suddenly grew worse. He
would frequently jump out of bed at night, rush to
the window struggling for breath. During the day he
was also often short of breath. Then he would stop
working and have mother take him for a walk. Up
to that time he had never rested during the day. Now
he always lay down for an hour after dinner. Grad-*

THE CASE OF MISS R.

ually he seemed to lose all interest in his family. Every now and then we heard him complain of being concerned about me. I gave no thought to the morrow, like a child, and there was no money in the house. Father felt that he did not have much longer to live and spoke of it, too. But I could not comprehend the seriousness of his disease. That he might die—I never thought of it. Soon he was hardly able to stand on his legs any more. Lina and the doctor had to give him injections which refreshed him for a while but the improvement never lasted long.

Father was very restless in bed. He could not live without his tailoring business. My sister was on vacation and nursed him. She and mother alternately sat up with him during the night. I always stayed awake until about eleven o'clock; then I grew so tired that I had to go to bed.

To protect himself from becoming cold, father wrapped a broad gray shawl around his chest. This shawl unfortunately belonged to the objects which I could not touch. I asked mother in vain to take something else for this purpose. She said that the shawl was just right. So I could not embrace and kiss father any more, which I wanted so much to do. I was even afraid to come near him; later on I regretted it many times although it was absolutely impossible for me to act differently.

For a short while it seemed he was going to recover

THE GOAL OF SUPERIORITY

in spite of everything. We put him in a comfortable chair and he told me a lot of funny stories of his boyhood. Every one laughed and we all hoped again. But the next day he was again in a somnolent state, sitting upright in his bed. I often saw him moving his hands in restless sleep as if he were sewing. One evening he arose suddenly, staggered to the sewing table in the kitchen and stretched out his trembling hands for a coat. We asked him to go back to bed. His feet were already swollen.

My parents were still not married. Mother was much troubled lest I remain an illegitimate child. When the doctor left her in no further doubt as to father's condition—I only learned about this afterward—and prepared her for the worst, mother talked matters over with Olga's mother. This woman ran straight for a priest. She learned from him that a marriage ceremony that evening at eight o'clock could be performed upon producing a certificate from a physician. Our doctor wrote out such a certificate. But it was difficult for mother to speak to father about the impending marriage ceremony. I remember her saying; "Look here, dear; you know we are not married yet—what will become of our Clara?" Father only murmured "yes" once in a while and nodded his head to what she said. When I heard that the ceremony was going to take place that very day I was glad despite my grief. At last—I was almost eighteen years

THE CASE OF MISS R.

old—I was going to be able to use father's name. Up to that time I had always told others that that was my name anyway. But now it really would be mine.

We bought two candles, borrowed a crucifix from a neighbor, a pious old woman, got some holy water, and put these things on a table covered with a white tablecloth. Everybody was very much excited. I trembled all over. At eight o'clock the priest came with the sacristan who had to serve as witness as well. During the ceremony Lina and I remained in the kitchen. Before leaving, the priest spoke to Lina and me and asked us to come to confession to him.

The ceremony exhausted father, especially since he had to confess and receive extreme unction at the same time. Mother wanted to make him believe he was not very sick. Completely spent he whispered that everything was all right but would she please spare him the sight of the priest in the future.

A few days later, I was visiting Minna in the evening, mother came into the room and said in a sad voice that I should go home with her as father was sinking. Mrs. K. accompanied us. Father was asleep, sitting up in bed. I sat down beside him quietly. His breath was heavy and slow. Then I stole away to the kitchen. From time to time mother came into my room. I did not know that the doctor had told her father would not live through the night. Suddenly I heard mother cry, "Father! Father!" I rushed into the

THE GOAL OF SUPERIORITY

room and could just see father falling back onto his pillows. Lina embraced him. He had taken his last breath. I threw myself over his bed, kissed him, called for him, begged him to forgive me. I did not want to let go of him. Lina had to carry me out. When I got to the kitchen I felt nauseated and vomited.

Again we see that she belongs to the type of person who responds to excitement by nervous disturbances in the digestive apparatus. All inner organs of a human being are supplied by a separate nervous system, the vegetative nervous system which is older in evolution than the central nervous system and was formerly supposed to be the seat of life. When we are joyous and our heart beats more quickly as a consequence, when we blush with shame, perspire with fear or have a stomach ache because we dread something, it is always due to the activity of the "emotional" nerves which have been correctly classified as the sympathetic nervous (N. sympathicus). There are cases where this vegetative nervous system is abnormally sensitive (an organ inferiority) and as a result it functions more strongly than usual. We might add, however, that the source of irritation lies in the psychic structure of such persons, in their style of life. In such cases a small irritation produces a great reaction in those organs which are attached to this nerve system —the heart, the bladder, perspiration glands or digestive apparatus—as in the case of this girl.

THE CASE OF MISS R.

In order to treat such disturbances successfully, it is necessary to go back to the psychic source and from that point, to change the patient.

If we find, as in this case, that the psychic tension is increased as a result of the super-strong desires of the patient we have to consider and change her whole style of life. This can be done only by strengthening her social feeling. Her private intelligence is transformed into common sense in direct proportion to the strength of her social feeling. She feels at home with and agrees to the problems of life with all its advantages and disadvantages and loses her anxiety. From now on she no longer lives in a hostile world and no longer depends for her self-esteem on the opinions of others. There, on the useful side of life, she feels herself a respected human being, and her feeling of inferiority is reduced to the point where it can be very well utilized as an impetus to useful accomplishments.

The room windows were opened, a candle was lit. We crouched in a corner of the kitchen side by side, weeping and unable to sleep. When Mrs. K. left us, a neighbor came to take her place. We lay down only at dawn. We were stiff all over. The next day, when I woke up, I felt as if there were a great weight on my mind. I went to father, stroked and kissed him and put his cover in order. He looked so peaceful, not at all like a dead man. At night the men came with a coffin, laid father in it and carried him away. We were

THE GOAL OF SUPERIORITY

afraid to sleep at home, so we slept for a few nights at Mrs. K's. Mother told us that she had had a vision of a skeleton two nights before father's death.

In the chapel at the cemetery I saw father for the last time. His body was not altered. I still could not believe that he was dead. I stood in front of the coffin and expected him to open his eyes.

I was always looking at father's work table. I could not comprehend his being dead. I thought he might only have seemed dead. Mother and I locked ourselves in the bedroom at night. Saturday night the key to this room broke; we could not open the door the following morning. Mother called for the janitor through the window and let down a cord on which to hang all sorts of keys. None of them fitted. Finally a plumber opened the door for us.

I longed terribly for father; I cried without ceasing. Frequently I woke up frightened in the middle of the night; I could not breathe and felt grieved to death.

We can feel with the girl how deeply the separation from the father disturbed her. As long as he lived he was the pedestal upon which she had built her triumph. From now on the mother has to replace him inasmuch as she is fitted for such a position.

Then I dreamed that a dog with a muzzle bored his snout into me and turned and twisted it around. It gave me an extremely painful sensation. I turned on

THE CASE OF MISS R.

the light and looked to see whether I was bleeding or hurt anywhere. But I did not find anything. This dream was repeated frequently.

I also dreamt many times of a tall, bearded man standing at the foot of my bed—and woke up frightened to death. I could see him as distinctly as if he were really there.

And then I saw in my dreams a flower rising slowly and bending toward me—one single flower with five leaves like fingers. Again I woke up full of anxiety.

One could only interpret these dreams correctly if the girl were to give us some information about her thoughts and remembrances in association with the dream material. However, we have two important supporting points. We know her life gait and the problems that oppress her and we can understand the mood emanating from her dreams. These dreams, correctly interpreted, should give evidence of the road which she is using as a bridge to her goal of superiority, away from the road of logic and common sense. And the moods springing from those dreams should also aim in the same direction.

In the first dream we find the problem of love as the present central problem in the life of this girl. Her aim is to escape union with a man. That the dog represents a man is a safe assumption. We frequently

THE GOAL OF SUPERIORITY

happen upon such a tendency to degrade in dreams. Since the girl has clearly demonstrated this tendency in former parts of her life story and since, as we have read before, she occasionally has called a man a dog, our assumption is certainly justified. The muzzle is a little confusing. But if we remember that she always endeavored to provide men with a muzzle, to play tricks on them, to eliminate dangers and evade possible consequences, our attention will be more strongly directed to the fact that her "yes-but" has not only had a reinforcement of the "yes" but also a reinforcement of the "but." The pain and the fear of being hurt, of bleeding, permit her to assume that no precautionary measure is sufficient.

The second dream, also frequently repeated, permits the conclusion that in the mood of the dream she is alone with a man. This man—by way of precaution—is not pictured as friendly, either. It is impossible to identify him at this place. However the second dream fairly confirms the conclusions drawn from the first dream.

The third dream is ambiguous. We should go only so far as to suppose that the situation represents a hand stretching out after her. Here again we find the threatening approach and purposive generation of anxiety which characterizes the life of this girl plainly enough as the life of a pampered child.

THE CASE OF MISS R.

Here the story ends and with it our analysis. I emphasized at the beginning of the book that we were not concerned here with the complete biography of a human being but only with a portion of a life story. We were more interested in seeking what we could extract from the material given than in the completeness of the story. In private consultations as well we learn nothing more than parts of life stories from which we must draw our conclusions. I have tried to give the reader a picture of the procedure followed in a psychological analysis. I want my reader to see how a psychologist armed with a store of experience listens to, apprehends, works over, and understands an ordinary and otherwise insignificant life story. The very unimportance and commonness of this biography is significant in illustrating how much a psychologist can get out of it.

A patient whose life is so confused can be cured only by thorough understanding of how the condition developed. It is, in addition, our task to give the patient that insight which we have won ourselves by means of experience and common sense. Such a procedure encourages him. It is necessary only to use common sense to understand. Since common sense is

THE CASE OF MISS R.

much rarer than the word implies one must beware, in attempts at analysis, of premature inferences. Superficial, mistaken judgments serve to discredit those who make them.

As I have said, I was much more concerned with the events and results of this partial biography than with the completion of the story. I fear, however, that that will not satisfy most of my readers. The human intellect strives toward fulfillment; an unfinished fragment stimulates the imagination to create for itself a suitable ending. As much as I should like to help the reader in this respect I know no more than he does. As I said in my preface I have never seen this girl. All that I know about her has been written by her and by me in the present book. She makes mention in the story only once of her present condition; namely, when she tells us that to this very day she still cannot bring herself to use certain street cars. It may be assumed from that remark that her compulsion neurosis has probably improved a great deal but has not entirely disappeared.

Experience also teaches us that when one has done a right-about-face and set foot on the road to normal conduct, one progresses along this road in the right direction as quickly as one retrogressed before in the wrong direction. Just as every step into a neurosis inevitably destroys courage, every step out of a neurosis builds up courage and with it strength and social feel-

THE CASE OF MISS R.

ing. And that is in accord with what I have heard about the writer of this story; namely, that in so far as she has been able to help herself without the aid of a psychologist she has freed herself of her compulsion neurosis, and is taking courageous steps to solve her difficult life problems. I shall leave to the imaginative power of my readers, to their psychological understanding and intuition to divine how.